Gift book donated by
Lysle Meyer, PhD
Minnesota State
University Moorhead

Rev. J. W. Appleyard.

THE WAR OF THE AXE AND THE XOSA BIBLE

The Journal of
THE REV. J. W. APPLEYARD

EDITED BY JOHN FRYE

C. STRUIK (PTY.) LTD., CAPE TOWN
1971

C. Struik (Pty.) Ltd.
Africana Specialist and Publisher

This edition is limited to 1 000 numbered copies.

THIS IS NUMBER ...181

ISBN 0 86977 001 2

Printed in South Africa by Gothic Printing Company Limited,
Fir Street, Observatory, Cape

Contents

	page
Introduction	vii
Introduction to Chapter I	1
Chapter I: Marriage and Kaffraria	5
Introduction to Chapter II	27
Chapter II: Colesberg	29
Introduction to Chapter III	35
Chapter III: The War of the Axe (i)	39
Introduction to Chapter IV	79
Chapter IV: The War of the Axe (ii)	81
Introduction to Chapter V	119
Chapter V: Umlangeni, and the Bible in Xosa	120
Bibliography	141
Appendix	145
Index	151

List of Illustrations

Rev. J. W. Appleyard . . . . FRONTISPIECE

Facing page

War Dance in a Fingoe Settlement . . . 36
(*from Graham V. Robinson—Scenes in Kaffirland*)

Kafirs on the Edge of the Bush 52
(*from Capt. W. R. King—Campaigning in Kaffirland*)

A Patrol at Ease 84
(*from Capt. W. R. King—Campaigning in Kaffirland*)

Burghers from Cape Town 100
(*from Capt. W. R. King—Campaigning in Kaffirland*)

MAPS

Fort Peddie 5
Eastern Frontier 1840-1860   (*Between pages* 44 *and* 45)

Introduction

Appleyard's *Journal* is remarkable as an accurate and eminently readable account of the war of the Axe (1846-47) on the Cape Eastern Frontier. The bulk of the text, chapters three and four, deals almost entirely with the events of the war, some of which Appleyard himself witnessed. It is the best account written by a civilian.

Stationed as he was in the centre of activity, Appleyard was able to gain an overall concept of the war. His intellect and ability to maintain a certain depth of information make the *Journal* more than a mere chronicle of details. His ability to write good English also helps to produce a palatable account of the war.

Two other topics on which the *Journal* has valuable information are the daily life of a missionary on the Frontier, and the evolution of Appleyard himself from an ordinary missionary into the translator and printer of the first uniform edition of the Bible in Xosa. With regard to the first, much of what Appleyard writes can be found in various forms in other journals and diaries of the time. His value in this respect is not to be underestimated, and he incorporates into his information comments on affairs in South Africa in general. We are made aware, for instance, of the struggle between the British and Boer forces for supremacy in Natal, and there are comments on affairs on the northern border of the Cape Colony where the two forces also came to blows.

"Appleyard's Bible" was until comparatively recently still in circulation and in demand. It was produced about thirty years after the first Wesleyan attempts at translation of the Scriptures into Xosa had begun. In the pages of the *Journal* we find references to Appleyard's development as a translator, to his taking over the printing establishment on the Frontier and to the final production of the Bible in Xosa.

Appleyard was a modest man and in many cases extra information is necessary in order to assess more accurately his own part in the events which he described. Footnoting is therefore rather full, and an attempt has been made to enhance, if possible, the value of his comments by providing background information.

The *Journal* should not be interpreted as a mere collection of entries in a manuscript. One is faced in its pages with some plot which works itself out. There is a theme and a conclusion, and if one takes both internal and external evidence into account, it can be said that the *Journal* has a unity which is not complete until the last page has been written.

Appleyard was, of course, obliged to keep a record of his activities. As a member of the Wesleyan Missionary Society, a paid preacher of that Society, he was "peremptorily required" to keep a journal and to "send home frequently such copious abstracts of it as may give a full and particular account of his labours, success and prospects."[1]

Few missionaries seem to have carried out this rule satisfactorily. They were annually examined on the subject at the District Meeting, and it is clear from the minutes[2] of these meetings that the rule was often ignored. Appleyard himself felt no remorse at not having made entries in his journal for several years at a time.[3]

The abstracts were to be sent to the Secretaries of the Society in London, about four times a year. Here again many missionaries erred, and Appleyard was one of them. He has only three references to the Secretaries.[4] It is not possible to ascertain whether he wrote more often, because the Society's correspondence from South Africa for this period has been lost.[5]

We must accept then that Appleyard was not conscientious in obeying this particular rule. If we consider that most of the *Journal* concerns information which would not interest the Secretaries in any case, (and that did not interest Appleyard's biographer, Rev. Thornley Smith) then we may conclude that Appleyard made entries concerning the war because he enjoyed doing so. It may be objected that the most acceptable explanation was that he was bored during the war, when his activities were greatly circumscribed, but his meticulous attention to detail, care for truth, and the sense of occasion with which he writes, belie such a conclusion.

There is a theme which works itself out in the *Journal*. Appleyard would have called it Providence. Slowly the intellectual side of the man becomes dominant. Appleyard was as much a convinced Christian in 1841 as he was in 1859, but the emphasis of his activity changes within this period. The preacher still preaches, but the builder of mission buildings and the visitor of kraals becomes the translator and printer of the Scriptures. By 1859 Appleyard had not only produced a Xosa Bible but had made a great and enduring contribution to the study of Xosa by producing an advanced grammar of the language.

His contribution to the service of his Lord was that of the mind rather than that of the mouth, and he was happier in this type of service. It took him some time to realise this. He had been well grounded in Latin, Greek and Hebrew at the Wesleyan training institution in England, and had begun the study of Syriac and Chaldee privately because he loved languages. On coming to Africa he neglected language studies for the practical work of the mission field.[6] Only in 1842 did he realise that there was scope for his interest within his vocation. The entry for 27 June 1842 is significant:

"I have been very busy since the District [Meeting] in compiling a Kaffer grammer (sic) according to my own views. I finished it last week, and intend to revise and improve it, if spared, next year when I hope to have a little more experience. I shall now commence a dictionary, Kaffer and English. These studies are by no means disagreeable to me, but appear just what suits my cast

Biographical information on J. W. Appleyard can be obtained in the Dictionary of South African Biography, Vol. I, and in T. Smith's *Memoir of Rev. J. W. Appleyard*. London, 1881.

Notes and References

1. Quoted in D. Williams: *The Missionaries on the Eastern Frontier of the Cape Colony, 1799–1853*, Appendix: rules of the Wesleyan Methodist Missionary Society.
2. Manuscript Minutes in Cory Library: MS 15,704; 15,023; 15,024, passim.
3. See the entry for 8 August 1853 (below, p. 131) and that for 25 June 1859 (below, p. 132).
4. See below, p. 8, 102.
5. See Hinchliff, P. B.: *Calendar of Cape Missionary Correspondence, 1800–50*, p. 255.
6. See below, p. 83.
7. An example: on p. 36–7 of Smith's *Memoir*, the following appears as part of the entry for 28 April 1843:
"This morning I met my class without an interpreter, and prayed with the members at the close in their own language, for the first time. My interpreter happened to be absent, and I thought I might possibly be able to say something to each of them . . ."
This extract is identical to that on p. 19, below, except insofar as "them" in the MS becomes "the members" in Smith's *Memoir*'

Introduction to Chapter I

Fort Peddie is situated about half-way between Grahamstown and King William's Town. It is also about half-way between the Great Fish River and the Keiskama River, both of which have served at different times as the official eastern boundary of the Cape Colony. It is "in line with two important crossings, Trumpetter's Drift [over the Fish] and Line Drift [over the Keiskama]".[1] Its strategic importance was such that during the second quarter of the nineteenth century it was the cockpit of the struggle for land and cattle between the "Kafir" tribes and the Colony.

The old fort or post is situated on the opposite side of the national road to the present town of Peddie and the original buildings have to some extent merged with the more peaceful atmosphere which pervades the neighbourhood to-day. The watchtower is almost merged in a copse of trees, the mud walls of the Star Fort have been flattened and the old Commissariat store which was contained within the walls has been adapted for the worship of the parish of St. Simon and St. Jude. The Infantry barracks has been entirely demolished and the Cavalry barracks is also threatened. The military hospital has been adapted for other uses. So has the parade ground – it is now a rugby field.[2]

Fort Peddie achieved prominence in the period 1836–1846. This was the period during which the Glenelg-Stockenstrom Treaty System was in operation. The frontier was officially the Keiskama but the Xosa tribes had recovered the land between that and the Fish with the exception of Fort Peddie and its environs.

The fort was established in 1835 and named after the commanding officer of the 72nd Regiment, which had served in the war of 1834–1835. The purpose of its erection was to protect the Fingoes who were a group of tribes once resident between the Drakensberge and the sea.[3] They had been decimated in Chaka's wars and the movements of tribes which had resulted from those wars and had taken refuge with the eastern branch of the AmaXosa tribes, the Gcaleka, under the paramount chief Hintza. Sir Benjamin D'Urban[4] had waged a short campaign against

Hintza and he supervised the exodus of the Fingoes to the eastern frontier of the Cape Colony in 1835. They were granted locations between the Fish and the Keiskama on 14 May 1835 and swore allegiance to the King of England. Rev. John Ayliff of the Wesleyan Missionary Society was their acknowledged mentor and he remained with them for a time at the request of the Governor. D'Urban established the garrison fort to protect them from the neighbouring tribes of western Xosa who had already made known their dislike of the newcomers.[5] The number of Fingoes who thus emigrated was estimated by Ayliff at 16,800 souls; of this number only about 2,000 were men. They brought with them about 22,000 cattle.[6] They established a body of "Chiefs and Council" to regulate their affairs.[7]

The tribes and their chiefs as in 1844 were: Njokweni, chief of the Zizi, Mabandla of the Bele and Ukwenkwezi of the Bele, Matomela of the Reledwane, Kaulela of the Imbuto, Umphala of the Ukunene, and Jama of the Kuze.

The area round Fort Peddie had long supported a heavy population,[8] and the arrival of the Fingoes greatly aggravated the position. D'Urban had also allowed the Gunukwebi tribes to remain in the area and the Ndhlambi tribes to return to it. The tribes and their component clans were not scrupulously divided into geographical areas but it may be said that the Fingoes were surrounded by many different chiefs and therefore had many potential enemies. To the south and south-east were the Gunukwebis under Pato, Kobus and Kama, and to the north-west, north and north-east the Ndhlambis under Umkye, Umhala and Seyolo. There can have been no doubt in the minds of the chiefs and their people that the Fingoes occupied land which had once been theirs and which they could hope to have again. It is no accident that the Gunukwebi chief Pato, who had kept his tribe out of the war of 1834–35, was the last to surrender to the British in the war of 1846–7.

The Glenelg-Stockenstrom Treaty System was a method of regulating contact between the Colony and the tribes based on the recognition of the tribal authorities as autonomous political entities. Colonial Diplomatic Agents were stationed with the Gaikas, Gunukwebis and Ndhlambis, one to each group of tribes. The Diplomatic Agent for the Gunukwebis was stationed at Fort Peddie and his house was about 200 yards to the south of the Star Fort.[9] His duty was to keep the peace between the Gunukwebis and the colonists and between the Gunukwebis and the other tribes, including the Fingoes. This he had to do largely through personal influence: he could not use the garrison or even native policemen in the execution of his duties.[10]

Something of the nature of life at the Fort at this time can be appreciated from the reports of one of the Diplomatic Agents. He was Theophilus Shepstone, later Sir Theophilus Shepstone, famous for his native administration in Natal and his annexation of the Transvaal. Apart from the regular troops who inhabited the Fort there were some civilians living there. It has not been possible to discover when they arrived, but presumably they were contractors of some description. Joseph Stirk, one of the emigrants of 1820, was among them.[11] The time came when the "Commanding Officer of the Engineer Department" ordered the white civilians off the post.[12] Stirk then applied for a grant of land adjoining the post and Shepstone addressed his request to the Fingoe Chiefs and Council, whose land he would be taking. We presume that Stirk received land, for Appleyard refers to him in terms that imply that he was familiar around the post.[13] After the war of 1846–7 when the area round Fort Peddie was thrown open to purchase by colonists as farms, Stirk and others associated with the post came to own the land on which they had been sojourners.[14] The first farm was granted to Richard Tainton, previously catechist at the Gwanga Wesleyan Mission Station, in 1849.[15]

There was by 1846 "a spirit of discontent at the whole Fingoe Settlement".[16] Pato complained that there were many Fingoes living on his tribe's land and Gunukwebi discontent was not alleviated when it was pointed out that some of Pato's men were living on the Fingoe reserve. The attitude grew among the authorities and even the missionaries that Pato was unreasonable, even treacherous, because of his hostility. Appleyard adopted this attitude with no misgivings.

Three Wesleyan Mission Stations were founded in the neighbourhood of the Fingoes in 1835. D'Urban Mission Station was built within a mile of the Watchtower at Fort Peddie. D'Urban was surrounded by one of the Fingoe locations which stretched down to the stream separating it from the Watchtower. The Beka (Begha) Station lay about five miles to the east of the Watchtower on the Begha river. It was established primarily to serve Kama's Gunukwebis but also Kobus and Pato's people in the area and the Fingoes.[17] Newtondale lay about 15 miles to the south and about three miles by road from the Fish River.

Two other stations feature quite prominently in Appleyard's narrative: Wesleyville and the Gwanga station.[18] The former was founded in the

1820's by William Shaw, and the latter in 1839 to cater for the Ndhlambi of Umkye's tribe who had moved from the Mount Coke area. Wesleyville was south-south-east of Fort Peddie and the Gwanga lay between the Fort and the Keiskama, in a northerly direction.

Notes and References

[1] N. C. Pollock and S. Agnew, *An Historical Geography of South Africa*, p. 77.
[2] Information supplied by Mr. J. M. Donald, 2 Military Road, Peddie.
[3] J. Ayliff, *History of the Wars causing the dispersion of the Fingoes*, Manuscript in Cory Library, Rhodes University, Grahamstown. Cory MS 15,544.
[4] Governor of the Cape from 1834-38.
[5] Ayliff ibid. p. 31.
[6] Ayliff ibid. p. 26.
[7] T. Shepstone to Agent General, dated Peddie 7 July 1844. Cape Archives L.G. No. 408 p. 8.
[8] cf. Report by Lieut. Ives Stocker in 1820. In G. M. Theal, *Records of the Cape Colony, 1793-1827*. Vol. XIII, p. 32 f.
[9] Information supplied by Mr. J. M. Donald of Peddie.
[10] T. Shepstone to Agent General, dated Peddie 1 May 1845. Cape Archives L.G. No. 408.
[11] For additional information on Stirk see E. Morse Jones *Roll of the British Settlers in South Africa*, p. 158 (includes photograph) and J. M. Bowker *Speeches, letters and selections from important papers*, p. 8.
[12] T. Shepstone to Agent General, Peddie 7 July 1844. Cape Archives, L.G. No. 408.
[13] See below, p. 111.
[14] Resident Magistrate to Lieutenant Governor, dated Peddie 1854. Cape Archives, L.G. No. 344.
[15] Mr. J. M. Donald in Supplement to the *Daily Dispatch*, 5 September 1960.
[16] T. Shepstone to Agent General, Peddie, 18 June 1845. L.G. No. 408 p. 25.
[17] Minutes of the District Meeting for the Albany and Kaffraria Circuits, 9 February 1836. Cory Library MS 15,704.
[18] The station was named after the stream on which it was situated.

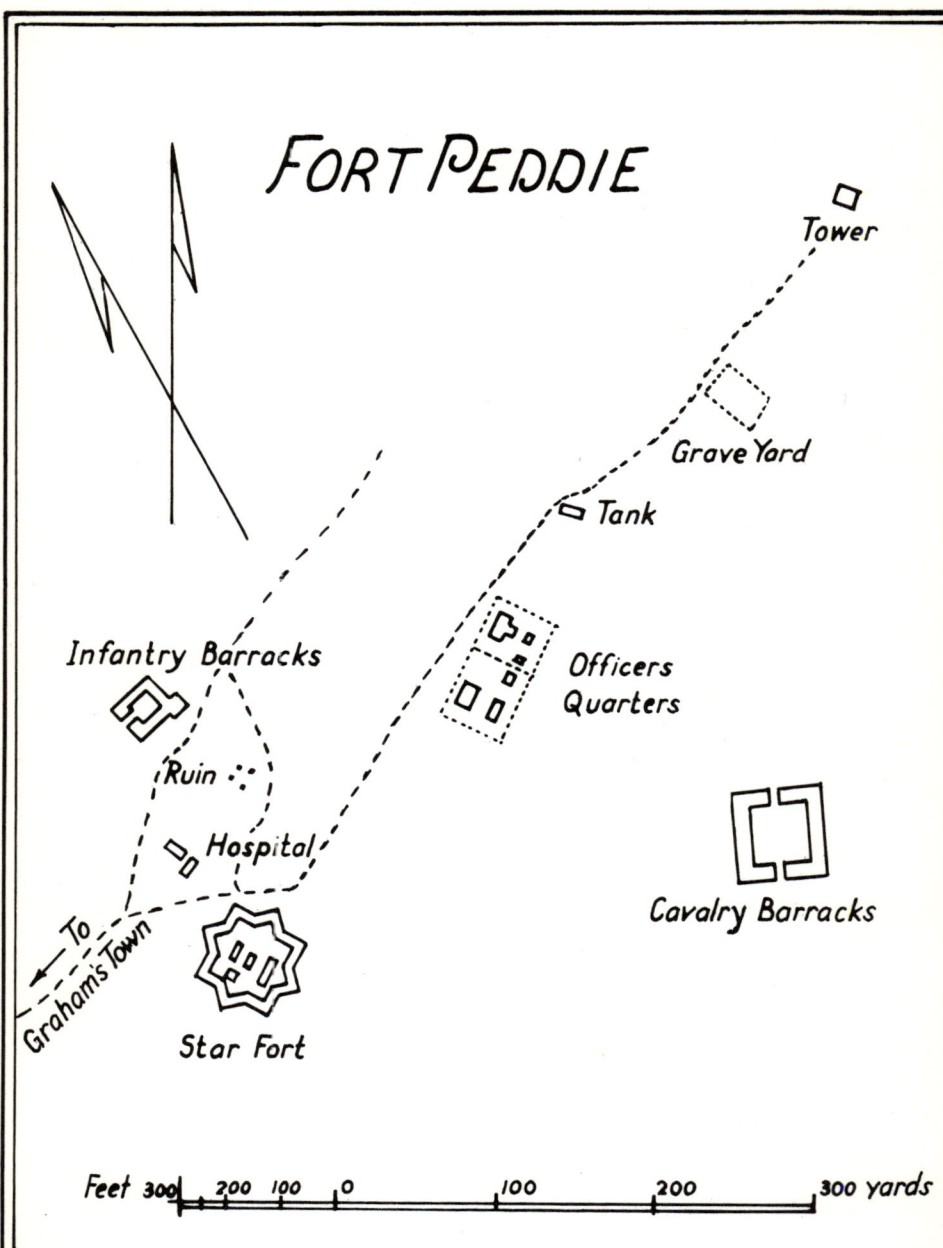

Chapter I

Marriage and Kaffraria

Tuesday April 13th: To-day forms the commencement of a new era of my earthly existence, having entered into the tenderest and most important relation of this present life – that of Matrimony. I was married in the Wesleyan chapel, Salem, Albany, South Africa, by the Rev. Mr. Shaw,[1] to my dearest Sarah Ann, eldest daughter of the Rev. James Archbell. After the ceremony, we sat down to dinner with a few friends, mostly missionaries and their wives, spending the remainder of the day, in the normal manner on such an occasion – And now may the God of our Fathers, cause his face to shine upon us, help us to do and suffer his righteous will, and grant us all spiritual and temporal blessings, through Jesus Christ our Lord – Amen.

Sunday April 18th: Heard Mr. Green[2] this morning and preached myself in the evening.

Tuesday April 20th: Left Salem this morning with my dear wife in Mr. Archbell's wagon, and reached Graham's Town at dark – Spent the evening at Mr. Boyce's.[3]

Monday April 26th: Arrived at the Beka this afternoon[4] – We left town on Thursday evening in two wagons, and overtook Mr. & Mrs. Impey[5] in the flat where we remained for the night – It rained almost incessantly, but did no further damage than to deprive us of our coffee. The next morning we started after breakfast, and slept near Fraser's camp.[6] On Saturday afternoon we climbed the Fish River hill & reached Newtondale in time for tea. Here we tarried the Sunday over, leaving it this morning.

Sunday May 2nd: Entered to-day upon the ministerial

labours of this Station. I held the morning school from 11 to 12 o'clock, and the afternoon from 3 to 4; holding two services in the interim. Although I understood scarcely a word I read, yet I managed to give out the hymns, and get through the prayers so as to be understood in the general. May the Lord assist me in the acquisition of the language of this people, that I soon may have it in my power to speak and preach in it! May He give me grace and wisdom to apply his word to their hearts, that they may understand and profit thereby!

Thursday May 6th: Rode over this morning to the Gwanga where we have an out-station connected with this. Mr. R. Tainton[7] is the Assistant resident there. It was established about 18 months since.[8] Umgai is the principal patronizing chief. After our return I held our week-day service, which most of our Station people attended, from about ½ past 2 till ½ past 3.

Friday May 7th: This afternoon I held our weekly class meeting. We have 14 members in all.[9] After meeting them I endeavoured to explain and enforce the rule respecting class & ticket money,[10] and desired them to pay what they could weekly. To encourage and incite them to this, at least the women, who complained of not having money, I told them that I would give them a penny every week if they would undertake to collect and bring to my house a bundle of wood, which would make the matter very easy for them. With this they seemed pleased.

Saturday May 8th: Rode out this morning to the neighbouring kraals to invite them to church on the coming Sabbath.[11] I visited Pato's, Kaloko's, Utyala's (brother of Kaloko) Xosa's and Utofili's (brother of Xosa) Kraals.[12] They had just slaughtered a beast at the great place and were busy preparing for eating. The breast, according to custom, was allotted to the chief and his great men, whom we found sitting under the fence of the calf kraal, whilst all his men were busy in the cattle kraal. Great slices of the beef were lying about on the fence waiting to be broiled on the fire which was kindling.

Sunday May 9th: Held the services as last Sabbath. Pato and some of his great men attended. Pato and Xosa dined with us.[13]

Friday May 14th: To-day we found a swarm of Bees lodged in a cluster on the bough of a thorn tree near the chapel. We brought the bough home and succeeded in shaking them off into a box, which we intend serving the place of a bee-hive.

Saturday May 15th: Rode another round to-day among the Kaffer kraals. Visited 12 of them, viz. Nkulu's, Ngxoya's, Ndamanti's, Ntambo's, Nkoli's, Falhein's bee place, Ungesi's, Ngyogyo's, Ukobo's (son of the late Balata), Uhoma's, Nondyola's, and Ngwa's.[14] At one of the kraals 2 Doctors[15] had just arrived. Some of the cattle were sick, and they had been sent for to cure them. I asked them to tell me their method of cure, that I might heal my cattle should they get sick. They replied, however, that they did not teach us.

Monday May 17th: To-day I received a box of various articles from England. It was sent from home last September, so that it has been nearly 9 months on the way.

Wednesday May 19th: This morning we succeeded in mounting our Station bell, which I brought from Town with me. In the afternoon a large flock of Locusts lodged on the hills a little distance from the Mission House. The ground was literally covered with them, giving it a reddish appearance.

Saturday May 22nd: Went out on another excursion to the neighbouring Kraals. Visited nineteen, viz: those of Ndywaro, Nmarantsi, Usali, Ngxumi, Umbe, Umyisheni, Umbulu, Utyutyu, Ukelembi, Ukobo, Umatoyi, Ugxehao's bee place, Ufani (or Uhobosho), Ungqera (the husband of Yoyoze, Pato's sister), Umbulula, Ngxasana, Ubuvu, Umatyumza, and Uvana. This afternoon rumours of war reached us. It seems that Pato and Umgai have found some cause for a rupture. But I trust that under the Divine blessing through British interference nothing serious will occur.[16] This evening I lost my faithful riding horse Caesar, by that mysterious disease termed Horse-sickness. He was taken last evening.

Monday May 24th: This morning I commenced a day school.[17] About thirty children attended, the greater number being girls. In the afternoon Mrs. A. began a sewing school for the girls, which she intends holding every Monday and Wednesday afternoon.

Monday June 7th: Mr. Archbell arrived here on Saturday on his way to Natal.[18] He left us this morning for Mount Coke. He intends spending the next Sabbath at Morley.[19] Mr. Davis[20] accompanied him from Town on his way to Butterworth. He preached for me on Sunday in Kaffer both times.

Tuesday June 8th: Spent the day at Peddie.[21] Mr. Impey had gone to Town. Called on Mr. Shepstone[22] and Mr. Hare.[23]

Friday, June 11th: Received letters from Mother, Sisters, and Cousin Sarah, dated Janry & Febry last. My brother, it would seem, has given up the idea of being a Wesleyan Minister, since which a young Clergyman has offered to pay all his expenses at Oxford, if he will enter the Church. And to this he seems inclined.

Tuesday June 15th: The Anniversary of my birth-day; having completed my 27th year. To God be all the praise for the mercies of these years of my life. May I spend the remainder, whether fewer or more, to his glory and good of his Church! Wrote home, also to Jno. Marn,[23] the Secretaries[24] & Mr. Wason[23]. A few days since I wrote to my Uncle.

Sunday July 11th: Administered the Sacrament of the Lord's supper to the Members of the Society.

Sunday July 18th: Preached in the morning at Ft. Peddie and in the afternoon at the Gwanga. Mr. Impey supplied my place at the Beka.[25]

Sunday July 25th: This morning Mr. Archbell arrived on

his return from Natal, which he left on Monday week last.²⁶ He was of course rather tired, but in other respects was quite well. He has been quite pleased with his trip. He found things even better than expected among the Boers. They gave him a hearty welcome.

Wednesday July 28th: The first Kafferland Quarterly meeting²⁷ was held at D'Urban to-day. Mr. Shaw presided. It consisted of the Missionaries and the Local preachers or Assistants of the 4 Border Circuits. The usual routine of a Quarterly and Local Preachers' Meeting was gone through as far as the Foreing (sic) work can be assimilated to the Home. No Financial business was done as that belongs only to the District Meeting.

Sunday August 1st: Preached at Ft. Peddie for Mr. Impey who is gone on to Wesleyville and Mt. Coke with Mr. Shaw.

Thursday August 12th: Returned this evening to the Beka after an absence of a week in the Colony. Saturday and Sunday I spent at Salem. On Monday I rode to the Farm with Mr. Archbell to get some cattle.²⁸ On Wednesday I rode to Mr. Birt's²⁹ of the London Missionary Society where I remained for the night.

Friday August 13th: Received a letter from my brother, who confirms what my sister said in her letter respecting the probability of his entering the Church.

Tuesday November 2nd: For the last three or four months I have been almost exclusively engaged in the erection of the outbuildings in order to complete the Mission premises, so as to render them convenient and comfortable.³⁰ They consist of a wagon house, stable, store & hen house and all built of mud.³¹ I have also made fruit garden between the house & chapel, so that the whole premises may be fenced in, snug and compact, which will be done as soon as the repairs of the house and chapel are completed. Thus the greater part of my first year's residence here is gone in almost totally temporal labours and engagements. The remainder, however, I hope to devote to the more especial part of my work. And may the

God of all grace grant me his abiding blessing that I may be successful in every undertaking for the promotion of his cause, and for the temporal and spiritual benefit of the people, amongst whom he has appointed me to dwell!

December 8th: Returned last evening from Wesleyville, whither we had accompanied Mr. Archbell & family on their way to Port Natal. They arrived here nearly three weeks since, spending about a fortnight with us. They went on yesterday to Mt. Coke, and intend reaching Butterworth early next week.

December 19th: Preached at Fort Peddie in the morning, as I did likewise on the preceding Sabbath, Mr. Impey having gone to Butterworth with Mr. Shaw.[32] After the service, I married a Hottentot couple. Returned to the Beka, and took the services here also. During the former one baptized three Fingoe children.

December 24th: Reached Jas. Archbells[33] farm on the Koonap this evening. We left the Beka in our wagon on Tuesday.

December 26th: Held a Dutch service with the Hottentot people on the place, who number about 30 including children.

1842

January 5th: Arrived in Graham's Town this afternoon,[34] having left the farm yesterday. The country seems generally dry in this province, as well as in Kafferland. The drought has been of several weeks' continuance, and fears are entertained of the failure of the Indian & Kaffer corn crops.[35]

January 9th: Preached this morning in the English chapel.

February 1st: Returned from Town last Thursday. The District meeting closed on the preceding Monday.[36] It was a long and busy one. My health was but very indifferent, during its sitting. Found all my crops totally destroyed in one way or other. In other respects, I found all as could be wished.

February 6th: Mr. Thomas[37] arrived here yesterday on his way home. He preached for me in the morning, and I catechized them in the afternoon on what they had heard.

Afterwards I published for our weekly services, viz. as follow:– Monday morning, a prayer meeting; Tuesday, a singing meeting; Wednesday, Preaching; Thursday, a catechumen class, and Friday, the class meeting. On Saturday I intend to resume my itinerating amongst the neighbouring Kraals. The greater part of last year was occupied in the temporal affairs of the Station, but now having brought all these to a tolerable finish, I intend, with God's blessing, to attend to the spiritual wants of the people by whom I am surrounded. And may God, in his infinite love to their awfully degraded souls, crown my every endeavour with success.

April 3rd: Since our return from Town, both Mrs. A. & myself have been the subjects of affliction. I was first taken with the yellow jaundice, and after recovery from that disease, I had inflammation on the lungs, which I took on an itinerating tour to the Sea-side, through lying a short time on the damp ground, whilst talking with some of the natives. However, I thank God that I am pretty strong again, except perhaps a little weakness in my chest. I preached twice to-day for the first time since my attack, and I trust that the Lord will preserve me in health, that I may be strong to labour in this part of His vineyard. The people are now in a very disturbed state owing to daily thefts which are taking place, – cattle being stolen by day & by night, and no one can tell by whom.[38] Strange rumours are afloat of the intentions of some of the other tribes, but I trust they may only prove rumours. May the Lord hasten the time when nation shall not go to war with nation, but when peace, – universal peace shall reign, in this & every land!

The following instance of superstition came under my own observation, and which is not uncommon amongst the natives in general. The person was my own herder. It appears that after I left for the District meeting, he fell sick and continued so for several weeks after my return. I kept him on the Station as long as he would stay, but not getting much better he went home and sent for one of their doctors. She plastered him with cow dung, and after it was taken off told his friends to cook with it — They found a bone, a piece of flesh, which was mutton, so she said, and some pieces of wire. All this he firmly believes the woman brought out of his body, though he could not see any marks — The woman told him that a certain person whom she named had bewitched him in this way, because he was liked too much by me, and therefore as soon I was gone, took the opportunity of causing these things to enter into certain parts of his body, that he might fall sick — The plain fact is, that the poor man was suffering chiefly from rheumatism — However he is so afraid of being bewitched again, that I cannot get him back to herd.

April 17th : Preached this morning at Fort Peddie in English. Also took one service here. Things in general look very discouraging at present. This tribe appears to be in a disturbed state — A few days since Pato & Kobi made an attempt upon Kama with the full intention of destroying him;[39] but by the timely interference of Mr. Shepstone, the resident agent at Fort Peddie, bloodshed was prevented — He has since sent for them to hear what they have to say about the matter — I fear that Pati is in league or about faring one, with the Gaika and Jlambi[40] chiefs, to make another irruption into the colony, if an opportunity should offer. But he knows that Kama will not join him, & hence perhaps his wish to remove him out of the way. It would almost seem as if some great crisis was upon the even of taking place with regard to Kaffer affairs in general. May such be made instrumental to the salvation of these wretched heathen!

May 12th: Returned from Fort Beaufort this morning. Preached there for Mr. Holden[41] on the past two sabbaths. Several rumours were afloat concerning the Kaffirs (sic). The farmers generally were very unsettled, being apprehensive of another Kaffar (sic) war. Utyali,[42] a Kaffer chief had died, and the people charged Suta, the mother of Sandilla with bewitching him, and according to Kaffer custom, she was to lose her cattle and to be burnt. Through the Lieutnt Governors influence, however, this is prevented, at least for the present.[43]

June 27th: Preached yesterday at the Gwanga, met the class for tickets, and administered the Sacrament of the Lord's supper. The congregations both there and here are very small, as they have been for some time past, owing to the excessive drought with which we have been visited for the last year. Most of the people have left this part of the country to procure grass and water for their cattle. And the few that yet remain are almost literally without food. It is almost incredible how little they appear to be able to live upon. May the Lord turn their hearts through this dispensation of his providence.

We have lately had awful and distressing intelligence from Port Natal,[44] whither Mr. Archbell proceeded last year, and where he arrived with his family the beginning of last month, only a few day (sic) before hostilities commenced. It appears that the small force, which was most imprudently sent a short time since to formally take possession of Natal,[45] is completely at the mercy of the Boers, who by their infatuated conduct, have shown themselves, rebels to their government. News has only reached us, as yet, of the night's attack in the bush,[46] and the next morning's seizure of the store on the landing place. Government has promptly sent succour, but it is generally thought to be far too small, as well as very imprudently commanded. The Governor has actually sent a Dutchman to fight his own kindred, a person, moreoever, who has never seen an action;[47] although he had others at his disposal duly qualified. It is now nearly a month since these things have occurred, and what has become of Capt. Smith and his little band in the interim time only can reveal. But it is generally supposed that they have been made prisoners. Mr. Archbell and family took refuge on board the Mazeppa, a schooner then lying in the bay.[48] But it is feared that the vessel [illeg.] has been taken, and all made prisoners. May the Lord preserve my dear relatives in this trying time, and give them peace and comfort and a speedy deliverance. May He also in great mercy so order this affair, that great good may be brought out of the evil!

I have been very busy since the District (sic) in compiling a Kaffer grammer (sic) according to my own views.[49] I finished it last week, and intend to revise and improve it, if spared, next year when I hope to have a little more experience. I shall now commence a dictionary Kaffer and English. These studies are by no means disagreeable to me, but appear just what suits my cast of mind. May the Lord assist me both to learn and speak the languages correctly, that I may be made the more effectually a blessing to those amongst whom it is my appointed lot to dwell!

July 3rd: Preached this morning at the Post for Mr. Davis, who has had an attack of the Jaundice, but is now recovering. Afterwards I preached here. The congregation is still but small. On Friday last we were favoured with a delightful rain of nearly twenty fours (sic) continuance. The consequence is that the Beka, which before was almost without water, is now abundantly supplied. We have water in almost all directions near our Station. I trust that this gracious visitation of Divine providence will not be lost upon the people.

No news from Natal, so that we have been in anxious suspense about Mr. Archbell and family for nearly a month. May the Lord preserve them in his abundant mercy!

August 8th: Preached yesterday morning at the Post and here. It appears that the Natal business has been settled, but the manner has not transpired. The general conduct of Col. Cloete seems to have given universal dissatisfaction, both to the military and civilians. Mr. Archbell and family escaped in the Mazeppa, after being plundered of nearly all his property,[50] to Delagoa Bay. He returned to Natal the day after the retaking of the Port by the troops sent round from Cape Town.

The Colonial government appear at length to be taking a decided stand against the Kaffers.

Two thousand head of cattle have been stolen from the border farmers during the past quarter alone. The Lieutt Governor[51] has given them 30 days to bring them back, and should they not have done so at the end of that time, he will send troops to take them.[52] This looks like decision at last, after six years of vacillation, during which the Kaffers have been permitted to steal almost with impunity by the government, to the no small injury and loss of the Colonial farmers. The Kaffers of this tribe and also of Zeno's[53] are the only ones, I believe, which are free from thefts which have not been paid for. This state of things affords sad reflection to the Missionary. They have scarcely any desire for the truth of the Gospel. They are ignorant and careless about it, and that wilfully. Their god is their cattle, and plunder is their prominent desire and endeavour. And those who are free from theft, are only free for want of a suitable opportunity, or in other words, they refrain from stealing, not from principle, but from fear of detection, or from policy. This is a dark picture, but nevertheless true with regard to the great mass of the Kaffer nations in general. Some change, therefore, in British policy towards them seems not only desirable but absolutely necessary, if the Colonists and Kaffers are to be preserved in friendly alliance.

September 21st: Returned home yesterday from Beaufort where I have been supplying two Sabbaths for Mr. Holden according to District appointment. Left home last Wednesday week for Peddie where I left Mrs. A.[54] On Thursday proceeded to Town. Spent Friday in Town, – part of the day in looking at the Library which makes a tolerable show.[55] They have a good selection of History. On Saturday went on to Beaufort. Sunday preached twice at the English chapel. On Monday went on to Fort Armstrong accompanied by Mr. J. J. Smith of the Commissariat. Preached there that evening, and at Post Retief the next. On Wednesday rode to Haslope Hills[56] through a very mountainous country ascending some thousand feet above the level of Beaufort. The drought was very evident, scarcely any goats to be seen. The Kat river settlement[57] looks very refreshing in distinction from the rest, as also the farms on the sources of the Koonap.

Much land was under cultivation with different sorts of grain, having the advantage of irrigation. On Thursday returned to Post Retief & went on to Kaal Hoek, and preached at Mr. Norris's.[58] Friday we returned to Beaufort where I preached in the evening. Also again on Sunday twice. Arrived at Fort Peddie about 10 o'clock on Monday morning having ridden through the night after 12. Thus the Lord hath continued his goodness to me through all my journeyings, and brought me home in peace & in safety. To Him be all the praise. During my absence one of our members has departed this life. His name was Bata. He was very deformed in his legs and was obliged for many years to walk by pushing on his feet with his hands. Latterly he had rather wandered in his mind and was continually in fear of being killed. I trust his release is a happy one for himself. He was formerly an Interpreter.

October 25th: Returned yesterday from the Sea-side.[59] Preached there on Sunday to about 50 Kaffers. I hope to be able to do this once now and then, as there are a great many people dwelling within a short distance of the place.

November, 4th: Rode to Fort Peddie this afternoon to baptize a child of Sargt. Harvey's[60] C.M.R. who was dangerously ill.

November 6th: Preached at Fort Peddie this morning. After the service I baptized the infant of Lieut. O'Riley,[61] named Fanny Ider. Returned and preached here.

November 13th: Preached again at Fort Peddie, and after service visited Sargt Smith[61] who was in a very precarious state. His affliction had led him to think of his spiritual state, and he had been especially moved to reflection in consequence of a fit which he had yesterday, through which he was nearly strangled. He therefore sent for me, and conversed on his state. I led him at once to the Saviour and showed him the necessity of heartfelt repentance. Here he felt his difficulty from his previous self-righteous notions, and wanted to know how he was to begin. I directed him therefore to those Scriptures which speak of our natural state and consequent duty, and hope from what he said, that his affliction will be sanctified to the salvation of his soul. I promised him to request Mr. Davis to call upon him, who would give him further advice and instruction. Afterwards I rode on to the Gwanga, where I preached to a good congregation of Kaffers. The chief N.Qeno[62] was there, and they were his people who were present. Na-Qayi[63] was absent at his bee place, and there was only one, I believe, of his men at Church.

November 16th: Mr. Shaw passed to-day on his way to Morley where he will hold a District meeting for that part of the District. He was accompanied by Mr. T. Smith[64] who intends taking a sketch of each of our Kafferland stations.

November 20th: Preached as usual on the Station this morning. In the afternoon, instead of holding the usual service, I rode out among the Kaffers. I went to a kraal where I heard they were eating meat, and found a few men sitting, after the repast, in the shade of the cattle kraal fence. They said that they did not know that it was the Sabbath, and pleaded hunger.[65] I had a long talk with them about their souls and some of their bad customs. They listened very attentively and entered into conversation. I think that their faith in some of their evil customs is greatly shaken. Pato was at the service this morning. I told him last night, that if he did not come to hear me in the church, I should come to him at his own place.

December 9th: Returned yesterday evening from the sea-side where we have been spending the last few days. On the Sabbath I held Divine service on the place, and afterwards visited a kraal where I heard they were meat-eating. The master of the kraal attempted to conceal himself for some time, but seeing at length, that he was only making matters worse, he confessed, and added that he had evaded our questions through fear, knowing that it was a great thing to break the Sabbath. I reproved him rather sharply, and at last he said, it was quite right, that I should thus visit them, for they needed frequent rousing.

December 18th: Preached this morning at Ft. Peddie. Returned and preached here. Afterwards married two couples, all resident on the Station, and one a member. The station made quite a show of European clothing, and the chapel was more crowded than I ever saw it before. I preached on the subject of marriage and pointed out the evil of polygamy and other customs arising from it. They spent the day in a very gratifying manner. On going to see them in the house which they had set apart for the feast, soon after my own dinner, I was pleased with finding them singing hymns, the feast having been conducted after English manner as far as possible.

1843

January 21st: Returned yesterday after attending the District Meeting in Town. We had a very pleasant and profitable time.[66] On Tuesday evening last, Bros. Holden, J. Smith,[67] T. Smith & self were ordained to the full work of the Ministry, having travelled our four years of probation at the last Conference,[68] with the exception of Bro. Holden, who has travelled five or six.

February 25th: Yesterday, sometime in the afternoon about 3 or 4 o'clock, my dear wife was confined of a little boy. Our Heavenly Father was very gracious unto us in this time of trial. Though my dear wife had been suffering violent paroxysms of pain all the day, & more or less the night too, yet we did not apprehend that she was in labour till a few minutes previous to her delivery, and then neither doctor nor nurse were at hand. But through the assistance of a Hottentot woman, and two or three Kaffer ones, my dear wife, did very well. Soon after the nurse arrived & at dark the doctor, and found all pretty well.[69] Thus is the Lord merciful to his servants in the wilderness.

March 15th: This morning between one & two o'clock, it pleased the Lord to take our dear little boy to himself. We had

spent the previous day at Peddie, and returned in the evening. He threw up some mucus at bed-time, together with his medicine; but afterwards seemed better and went to sleep as usual. About 11 or 12 o'clock, however, he gave a sudden scream, and appeared suffering from danger of suffocation in his throat. A warm bath seemed to relieve him for a little, but afterwards he went off in a dose, with an occasional gasp. When we gave him up as not likely to live, I baptized him with the name of John Archbell. Thus it has pleased the Lord to take our first-born from us, and thus cut short in their bud, the pleasing prospects which we had fondly anticipated. But "the Lord gave, and it is the same Lord who hath taken away", and therefore I will not murmur, but still bless and thank His holy name. My dear wife feels her loss very much, but I trust the Lord will make us both resigned, so that we may ever say, "It is the Lord, let Him do as seemeth Him good."
April 8th : Returned from Fort Beaufort yesterday afternoon. We started about three weeks since and passed through Graham's Town on our way. When we arrived at the Fish river near Fort Brown we found it full, and we had to stay on the banks between five and six days, including one of the Sabbaths I intended to spend at Beaufort.
April 28th : This morning I met the class without an Interpreter, and prayed with them at the close in their own language, for the first time. My Interpreter happened to be absent, and I thought I might possibly be able to say something to each of them, however short. And having thus commenced I intend to go on without the help of an Interpreter, reserving his assistance in the article of preaching alone.[70]
April 30th : Preached at Fort Peddie to the troops this afternoon in the open air, as there were too many for the usual place of worship to accomodate. In the evening Um-Hala[71] paid us a visit with his brother and two counsellors. He said he was on his way to Fort Peddie with about 90 of his people to see the Lieutnt Governor, who had sent for him.

An instance of gross superstition occurred at one of the

neighbouring kraals a short time since. It appears that the master of the place was sick, and, after some time, the doctor was sent for as usual. He said that the sick man was bewitched by an elephant in the bush, whose path he must have crossed at some time or other. He must therefore sacrifice two fat bullocks to this elephant, and then the sickness would leave him. This was accordingly done much to the satisfaction of the neighbours, who were all suffering from hunger as well as the doctor himself.

July 19th: Made my first attempt at preaching in Kaffer this evening. I took up the history of Abraham, the narrative style being the simplest.[72] I hope therefore soon to be able to do without an interpreter at all. May the Lord assist me by his wisdom to speak forth the words of truth and sound doctrine!

September 12th: Returned yesterday from Fort Beaufort and Mount Coke, having been absent from home four weeks. We have lately had a great deal of rain, which has of course altered the appearance of the country considerably.

November 17th: Returned from a short itinerating excursion to the sea. Preached at Kobus' place yesterday morning, and at the sea this morning. But most of the people were away at the dancing which is now going on throughout the country, on account of the individuals and places which were proscribed during the time of the small pox.[73] It is said that they have never yet been reinstated officially in their former privileges, and this therefore is designed to do it. Of course slaughtering is the principal means employed in cleansing the country, and several cattle have been slaughtered already in this neighbourhood, which is so far good as it feeds the hungry.

November 26th: Hearing that Pato was going to race cattle and have a dance to-day, I went to see for myself as soon as our morning service was over at the Station. As I approached the great place I saw that the thing was too true. I went up to the chief and reproved him. He pleaded ignorance of the day, and at my request immediately stopped the dancing. I then assembled the people and had a large congregation of Kafirs (sic) from all parts, and having read all the Commandments, preached from the fourth, as being particularly applicable to their circumstances. They were very attentive, and I trust this event will have a good effect.

November 28th: Pato called to-day, and I had a long conversation with him on the subject of his Sabbath law. He promised to send word to his people again, as also to attend the Church better than he had done lately.

December 3rd: To-day we had a noble congregation in the Church, and I was greatly encouraged.[74] Oh that the Lord would now begin to pour out his Spirit on this people! Darkness sits heavy all around, but the word and Spirit of the Lord can remove it all. O Lord! hasten the time.

Notes and References

[1] Rev. William Shaw, 1798–1872, founder of the Wesleyan Missionary effort in the Eastern Cape and General Superintendent of Wesleyan Missions in South Africa. All subsequent footnotes will name the Society to which a preacher belongs only if it is not Wesleyan.

[2] Rev. G. H. Green, ?–1887, appointed to the Salem Circuit by the District Meeting of 16 February 1841.

[3] Rev. W. B. Boyce, 1803–1889, attached to the Graham's Town Circuit. Boyce was author of *Notes on South African Affairs* and the Kaffir Grammar of 1834.

[4] Appleyard was appointed to the Beka and Gwanga circuit in 1841.

[5] Rev. W. Impey, ? – ?, appointed to the D'Urban and Newtondale circuit in 1841.

[6] This old military post lay about 30 miles from Graham's Town by road. See James Wyld's map, *Grahamstown and Outposts*. They would have crossed the Fish River at Trumpetter's Drift.

[7] Richard Tainton, 1797–1862. E. Morse Jones, *Roll of the Settlers*, p. 160 gives a sketch of the life of Tainton, who was a Settler of 1820. There is a photograph of Tainton and his wife in G. E. Cory *Souvenir of the Centenary of the 1820 Settlers* p. 86. Tainton was at this time in charge of the Gwanga Station under Appleyard's supervision.

[8] The Gwanga station was commenced in November 1839 to cater for Umkye, a Ndhlambi chief who had moved with his tribe from the Mount Coke area recently to "the portion of the Neutral Territory granted to him in 1836 by the Colonial Government." District Meeting, Minutes 1 April 1840. Cory Library MS 15,018.

[9] This number refers to members of the Wesleyan Missionary Society. It fluctuated from year to year.

[10] Church members were grouped into classes under a leader, and these met weekly. The "ticket" was handed out quarterly and recorded financial contributions. It allowed the holder to take communion.

[11] Missionaries were expected to visit "towns, villages or plantations in the neighbourhood of each Station", and their activities in this regard were investigated at the annual District Meetings. This Quotation is extracted from one of the questions put to each District Meeting.

According to a rule made by the Meeting of 1 April 1840 a travelling allowance of £1-0-0 p.a. was available to defray the costs of such visits. Each Missionary had a complement of three horses, valued at about £25. Expenditure to the amount of £10-0-0 p.a. was defrayed by the Society for saddlery and other accoutrements. Catechists like Richard Tainton were allowed from 50 to 75% less.

[12] Gunukwebi chiefs and heads of kraals.

[13] This was not without precedent. The Missionary at the Beka in 1837, William Shepstone, attributed the rapid expansion of his work as being partly due to the support of Pato and his councillors. Minutes of the District Meeting of 1838. Cory Library MS 15,704.

[14] Heads of kraals.

[15] i.e. witch-doctors.

[16] It did not lead to war.

[17] There had been such a school at the Beka as early as 1837, with an average of 50 children attending. Sunday School attendance had been 90. Minutes of District Meeting of 1838. The sewing school seems to have been an innovation.

[18] Appleyard's father-in-law Archbell had long wanted to go to Port Natal, "and as a considerable body of the Dutch farmers have often expressed a wish that he should be appointed to that country promising to aid considerably in his support", the District Meeting of 16 February 1841 had decided that he should go. He was to serve the Dutch, English and especially the Zulu populations. Before taking his family to Natal he went on an exploratory visit and it is this visit which is mentioned here. The cost of removal of the Archbell family to Natal was estimated by the District Meeting at £40.

[19] Mount Coke is near the present King William's Town and there is a large Mission Hospital there to-day. Morley was across the Kei river on the Umtata river. They had been established by Shaw in 1827 and 1829 respectively.

[20] Rev. W. J. Davis, 1810–83. He was an active translator into Xosa, especially of school textbooks. He was stationed at Butterworth, near Sirili's kraal, in 1841.

[21] There was an "English congregation" of 40–50 members at Fort Peddie as early as 1837. For them there were two Wesleyan services per week. There was one service per week for Hottentots at the Fort.

[22] Theophilus Shepstone, the Resident Agent. His house was situated about 200 yards to the south of the Star Fort. Oral communication by Mr. J. M. Donald of Peddie.

[23] unidentified.

[24] The Wesleyan Missionary Society required of each of its preachers that he write at least four times p.a. to the Secretaries of the Society in London. This rule was not always complied with. Instructions and other communications from the Secretaries were considered each year at the District Meetings. cf. Minutes of the District Meeting of 1 April 1840.

[25] Missionaries were instructed to exchange pulpits at least once per quarter with the preacher nearest them.

[26] In a letter to the *Graham's Town Journal* Archbell described his journey as follows: "The distance of Natal from Graham's Town is by land something more than 600 miles, as seventeen days' ride, averaging at least thirty-five miles per diem, brought me to the Dutch camp at Umlazi, eight miles from the post (at Port Natal)." Quoted in J. Bird *Annals of Natal 1495–1845*, Vol. 1 p. 652.

[27] A Quarterly Meeting was of more limited jurisdiction than a District Meeting.

²⁸ Presumably a farm belonging to James Archbell, son of Rev. J. Archbell, and Appleyard's brother-in-law. See below, note 32.
²⁹ Rev. R. Birt, of the London Missionary Society.
³⁰ In 1837 a brick chapel 50' by 19', and a "substantial brick dwelling house" had been completed. Minutes of the District Meeting 1838. Each Missionary (Preacher) on being appointed to a circuit in "Kafferland" was allowed the sum of £15 "in lieu of all claims for outfit of Crockery, Cooking Utensils, Bedding and all other Miscellaneous expenses connected with furnishing his house . . ." It is not clear from the Minutes whether the Preacher left his furnishings behind on being transferred to another circuit, but any inadequacy which he found in a new circuit was supplied by the Society. This applied only to certain items, including:
"four tables, nine chairs, one settee and mattress, two bedsteads, one chest of drawers, one wash stand, one fender, one looking glass in frame, one small ditto, eight flat irons, four bedroom candlesticks, two sitting room ditto, and one Kitchen Trivet."
Minutes of the District Meeting, 1 April 1840.
³¹ Extract from the Minutes of the District Meeting of 1 April 1840:
"*Waggon-House & Stables*. A Wagon-House & Stable is allowed to be erected on each station after the other buildings are completed. They shall be built with brick or stone walls and properly roofed and thatched, the sum to be expended in this way not to exceed £8 for each building or £16 for both . . ."
Enclosures or Fences. Resolved, that a substantially built wall of Brick or Clay, or Stone & Mortar, be allowed on each Station, as a Fence to the Mission Field & Gardens. The sum to be expended thereon not to exceed £15–0–0. for wh: amount a wall must be erected, not less than 500 yds. long, 5 feet high, and two feet thick on the average."
³² They went to attend the District Meeting of the eastern section, which began on 15 December 1841 at Butterworth. This was the first sectional district meeting, it having been decided at the joint meeting in February to make the Kei river the boundary between the two sections. Impey attended this meeting in an unofficial capacity. Minutes of the Annual District Meeting (Eastern Section).
³³ James Archbell, Appleyard's brother-in-law.
³⁴ He attended the District Meeting for the western section which began on 12 January 1842.
³⁵ Indian corn is maize and Kafir corn is a type of millet.
³⁶ During the proceedings of this meeting Appleyard was "received into full connexion" or accepted as a full-fledged Missionary.
³⁷ Rev. J. S. Thomas, ?–1856, stationed at Wesleyville. Thomas was murdered on his station at New Beecham Wood.
³⁸ In his report to the District Meeting of 11 January 1843 Appleyard claimed that this kind of disturbance adversely affected his work during 1842. The drought was another factor which caused some of his congregation to move away.
³⁹ The attempt on Kama did not lead to serious hostilities.
⁴⁰ i.e. Ndhlambi.
⁴¹ Rev. W. C. Holden, 1814–97, stationed at Fort Beaufort. Later a pioneer of Methodism in Natal and author of *History of the colony of Natal*, etc.
⁴² A son of Gaika and brother of Makomo. He died on 1 May. The case was involved and obscure.
⁴³ See G. E. Cory, *Rise of South Africa* Vol. IV p. 360–61.
⁴⁴ This news may have been carried by Dick King. On his famous ride from Port Natal to Graham's Town King received aid from Wesleyan Missionaries "at the different stations". J. Bird, *Annals of Natal 1495–1845* Vol. 1 p. 728.

[45] Under Capt. T. C. Smith.
[46] Capt. Smith's report of this reverse is found in Bird's *Annals of Natal* Vol. 1 p. 709-12. The attack began on the night of 23 May at 11.00 p.m. Smith's elaborate plan of attack failed. The Boer force was not taken by surprise and drove off the British attack. Smith had to abandon two guns. His losses were 16 dead, 31 wounded and 3 missing. The Boers immediately attacked the British camp.
During the negotiations before and after the battles Archbell acted as go-between.
[47] Lt.-Col. A. J. (later Sir Abraham) Cloete, 1794-1886, son of Hendrik Cloete of Constantia and Stellenbosch.
[48] The Boers had taken prisoner the captain of the Mazeppa, Allen. At the beginning of June the Boer commandant, A. Pretorius, allowed the British women and children and "all the English who did not belong to the troops" (Bird *Annals* Vol. 1 p. 730) aboard the Mazeppa. Archbell and family were also on board when Joseph Cato slipped anchor on 10 June and ran the Mazeppa past the Point. Cato sailed the Mazeppa successfully to Delagoa Bay in search of a British ship. He did not find one and returned to Port Natal safely on 27 June, one day after Smith had been relieved. G. E. Cory, *Rise of South Africa* Vol. IV pp. 148-153.
[49] The District Meeting did not officially instruct Appleyard specifically to engage in this work. It is likely, however, that he had already gone beyond Boyce's "Euphonic Concord" and formulated his idea of the possibility of correlating phonemes in Xosa. See Mr. J. v.d. Poll's article on Appleyard in *Dictionary of South African Biography*, Vol. I.
[50] In a letter written by Archbell to W. Shaw, dated Port Natal, 3 July 1842, he states that he had been subject to the confiscation of his stock and wagons and even his clothing. Cory Library MS 15,445.
[51] Lt. Col. J. Hare, Lt. Governor, August 1838-September 1846.
[52] Nothing of consequence resulted.
[53] Eno or Nqeno (Qeno).
[54] Mrs. Appleyard, his wife.
[55] The Graham's Town public library had been established in 1841.
[56] Haslope Hills was established by Shaw in 1837 as a village for freed apprentices. The apprenticeship of ex-slaves ended in December 1837.
[57] Established in 1828 on the initiative of Andries (later Sir Andries) Stockenstrom, as a settlement for Hottentots.
[58] Unidentified.
[59] Appleyard's circuit extended to the coast.
[60] There is an "Ensign Harvey" of the Cape Mounted Rifles mentioned in T. Gutsche *The Microcosm* p. 90.
[61] Unidentified.
[62] See above, note 53.
[63] Presumably Umkye.
[64] Rev. Thornley Smith, 1813-91, attached to the Graham's Town circuit. Biographer of Appleyard.
[65] During the 1830's Pato, **Kobus and** Kama accepted as binding upon them and their people the Wesleyan rule that there should be no feasting or dancing on the Sabbath. In 1837 Pato had fined several kraals for non-observance of this rule (Minutes of the District Meeting of 1838), but he was growing lax in this regard.
[66] Appleyard agreed at this District Meeting to produce "a series of Scripture Biography" for the "Quarterly Kaffir Periodical" of which Rev. H. H. Dugmore was then editor.
[67] Rev. J. Smith, ? -1876.
[68] The reference here is to the British Conference, the governing body of British

Wesleyan Methodism, which met annually and considered all candidates for the ministry.
[69] The nurse and doctor cannot be identified. There is no record of the Society employing medical staff at this period in this District. They probably came from Fort Peddie.

The following extract from the Minutes of the District Meeting of 1 April 1840 may serve to explain some of Appleyard's apparent carelessness with regard to childbirth:

"Lying-In"

"The allowances for Lying-In Expenses shall be as follows:-

Ist When the Dist. Midwife is in attendance .. .. £1-1-0.
II   When the Dist. Midwife cannot attend .. .. £5-5-0.
III When in the Colony on official duties, the usual Colonial
     allowance of £7-10-0

n.b. It is to be understood that the brethren deem it very undesirable that any Preacher in Kaffraria should visit the Colony for the purpose of his wife's confinement at G.Town or elsewhere . . ." If the Preacher disregarded this warning he would receive no allowance at all.

[70] This was regarded as a great step forward. For the disadvantages of using an interpreter, see P. J. Schutte, *Sendingdrukperse in Suid-Afrika 1800–1875*, pp. 161–3. Unpub. D.Phil (Bibl.) thesis presented to Potchefstroom University, 1969.
[71] Umhala was a Ndhlambi chief, son of Ndhlambi and brother of Umkye.
[72] The subject probably coincided with his work for the Quarterly Kaffir Periodical. See above, note 66.
[73] For details see *Wesleyan Missionary Society Reports*, 1842: Impey reported from Newtondale on an outbreak of smallpox in the neighbourhood and the "rigid system of quarantine" imposed. I am indebted to Mr. J. M. Berning of Cory Library for this reference.
[74] A direct result of Pato's renewed interest. Appleyard's report to the District Meeting of 1843 reveals strong emphasis on the influence of the chiefs at both the Beka and Gwanga stations.

Introduction to Chapter II

Appleyard was moved to Colesberg, in the separate District which covered the Bechuana Missions, in January 1844. He maintained contact with the Albany and Kaffraria District through the General Superintendent, William Shaw.

Colesberg was quite as colourful as the Eastern Frontier. It had been included in the Cape Colony in 1824 and was famous by 1844 for its wool, horses and high death rate. Its inhabitants had a reputation for drinking deeply,[1] and it had the lowest number of Wesleyan adherents of all the Bechuana circuits.[2]

The census figures for 1841 show a relatively high number of whites (about 4,200) and sheep (873,104).[3]

Appleyard was in Colesberg during stirring times, but the alarms and excursions around the Orange River find little echo in his *Journal*. The clash between the British and Boer forces in 1845 arose out of the tussle between the emigrant Dutch farmers and the Griqua people, who were protected by Britain, over land and jurisdiction in trans-Orangia.

First in this area had been the Griquas who had been settled, to some extent, by missionaries of the London Society after the turn of the century. Dr. John Philip, Superintendent of the London Society, had induced Adam Kok II in 1825 to live with his band at Philippolis,[4] only about 40 miles from Colesberg, but turbulent days lay ahead.

Other settlers were moving in. Kok's location was in the path of the Trekboers from the Colony who, as early as the 1820's, had begun a "systematic annual migration"[5] to the grazing lands north of the Orange. Soon they began to settle permanently. By 1843 there were already more Boers between the Orange and the Modder rivers than there were Griquas.[6] By that time one of the Great Trek commandants, Mocke, who had been disappointed in Natal had returned to trans-Orangia with the idea of creating an independent Boer republic there. At one stage the choleric Judge Menzies of the Cape bar, while on circuit in Colesberg, crossed the Orange and annexed the area in the name of Queen Victoria. He had not been authorised to do so, and when the Governor rescinded the annexation he sent a force composed of part of the 91st Regiment and a company of the C.M.R. to Colesberg, the closest point of British authority, as a deterrent to further violence. But matters grew worse and in 1845 flared into open battle between the Boers and the Griquas. The British troops brought about a temporary settlement at the skirmish of Zwartkopjes in 1845.

Notes and References

[1] T. Gutsche *The Microcosm*, p. 72.
[2] See the Minutes of the Bechuana District Meetings. Cory Library MS 15,001 (1).
[3] T. Gutsche, ibid. p. 77.
[4] J. S. Marais *Cape Coloured People* p. 40 & 41.
[5] J. S. Marais, ibid. p. 52.
[6] J. S. Marais, ibid. p. 52 quoting G. M. Theal.

Chapter II

Colesberg

1844

March 11th: The principal part of the last two months has been spent in attending the District meeting and travelling.¹ Arrived at Colesberg the second of this month, after nearly three weeks journey from the Beka.² Passed through Fort Beaufort and Cradock, at each of which places I spent a Sabbath. We are now nearly 300 miles to the North west of Graham's Town, and about 200 miles south of our Bechuana Stations.³ My work at present is confined to the English, amongst whom we have an interesting field of labour, though a limited one in point of numbers.⁴ I hope soon to acquire the Dutch language,⁵ and by that means to extend my usefulness. The Kaffer I am sorry to find will be of no use to me in this place, though I hope to succeed in finding out some, at the neighbouring farms, who speak and understand it.

A few days before our District meeting I finished my Kaffer grammar,⁶ which has occupied most of my time and study during the past year.

March 20th: Returned from Mr. Nelson's⁷ farm, where I preached Monday evening.

March 25th: Rode to Mr. Norval's⁸ farm, near the Orange river, and preached in the evening to his family and English workmen.

March 26th: Rode to the Orange river in the morning, and saw the float, which Mr. Norval has constructed for the purpose of taking across wagons, cattle, &c when the river is full. It is a simple and well-adapted contrivance, and brings him a good return. On my way home took breakfast and dinner at Mr. Gideon Joubert's,⁹ a respectable and worthy Dutch farmer.

August 4th: Commenced preaching this afternoon to the Troops stationed here, in consequence of the death of the Rev. Jas. Murray[10] the acting chaplain. He died early on Friday morning, and in the course of the day major Campbell[11] called on me to know if I would undertake the duty, and which I consented to do.

August 29th: Returned yesterday evening from Mr. Kolbe's,[12] who lives near the Stormberg Spruit, and where I preached last Sunday. He was formerly a missionary of the London Society, but for the last few years he has lived where he now is as a farmer. He has rendered himself famous among the Dutch for his medical skill, who flock to him from all parts to have the benefit of his advice. By this means he has generally a good congregation on the Sabbath, and is now anxious that we should take up the place, and build a chapel.

November 17th: This morning Bro. F. Taylor departed this life in great peace.[13] He came to Colesberg last April from the Interior in the last stage of consumption. He bore his long affliction with fortitude and resignation.

November 18th: To-day I performed the melancholy duty of burying the remains of our departed brother. Afterwards I took Mrs. Taylor and her three little children to our house.

December 16th: This evening Mrs. Taylor left us for Graham's Town, preparatory to returning home to her friends in Scotland.

1845

February 28th: Returned from our District meeting, which was held at Lishuani.[14] We left home the last Monday in January, and had a pleasant journey upon the whole, both going and returning. An opportunity was thus afforded us of seeing most of our own Stations as well as some of the Paris Society.[15] All appeared to be in a very encouraging state, though some more so than others.

April 6th: Rev. R. Giddy[16] preached for me to-day on his return from Graham's Town, whither he had gone for Financial purposes.

April 20th: Revd. Mr. Thompson preached for me in the evening. He is the resident Missionary of Philipolis, where disturbances have arisen between the Griquas and the Boers, and which have rendered his temporary removal necessary. These disturbances have called for the interference of Government, and the troops are now lying at the River,[17] waiting for orders from Head-quarters.

June 2nd: Mr. Archbell has been paying a visit to Graham's Town & Cape Town the last few weeks, but owing to our distance from both places we have been disappointed of seeing him. He wishes us to come to Natal next year, but it appears that the Brethren deem it necessary to send some one else.

The disturbances of the Boers are nearly brought to a close. The Governor is shortly expected. Our little cause has suffered from the excitement & other circumstances attending these disturbances. Two or three of our members have fallen into sin, and are no more of us.[18] Our week-night congregations are very small, and there is a lamentable indifference to religion abroad.

August 18th: All the troops engaged in the late disturbances have now left us, including those of the 91st Regt. We have now a company of the 45th. under Capt. Seagram,[19] consisting of about 104 men. My services, however, as Chaplain, have ceased, and the Capt. reads prayers to them on parade.

September 7th: This morning some of the 45th. were marched to our morning service, which is to be continued on each succeeding Sabbath.

September 11th: Returned from a short excursion to Phillipolis, (sic) distant 36 miles. The town or Mission station consists of one street of brick houses, the church standing at the top. At present the place is suffering from drought as well as from the late disturbances, so that most of the Griquas are now living at out-posts.

September 21st: Preached our S.S. Anniversary sermon this evening. Some of the children recited Scripture and poetry,

and others were examined in our Second Catechism.[20]
December 2nd : Returned last evening from Kamastone where our District meeting was held last week.[21] According to the present arrangement I am to return to the Beka. My removal will not take place, however, till after the Graham's Town meeting.

1846

January 29th : Received intelligence from the District meeting.[22] My appointment for the Beka is confirmed. Mr. Smailes is my successor here, and Mr. Holden[23] goes to Cradock. All being well, I intend leaving Colesberg in ten or twelve days.

Notes and References

[1] The time spent in travelling was felt by the Wesleyans to be largely wasted. cf. Minutes of the Albany and Kaffraria District Meeting 16 February 1841: ". . . it has happened that brethren have been unavoidably absent three months from their station by attending the District Meeting." Appleyard's journey was complicated by the fact that he was moving to a new circuit.

[2] By resolution of the District Meeting of 17 January 1844 Appleyard was moved to Colesberg: "In consequence of Bro. Taylor's having become supernumerary in the Bechuana Districts, it is found necessary to remove one of the Brethren to that District. We have therefore appointed Br. Appleyard to Colesberg, & Bro. Holden has been appointed to succeed him." For Rev. Taylor, see below note 13.

[3] The first "District Meeting of the Preachers of the Bechuana District" was held in January 1838, and by 1844 the new District included Thaba 'Nchu, Ratabane, Metumetsu, Platberg, Lishuani, Umpukani, Imparani, Levumilo, Moteng, Colesberg and Kamastone. Cory Library MS 15,001 (1).

[4] There were fewer men and women attending church in Colesberg than in any other circuit in the District. Appleyard preached five times per week and conducted one weekly prayer meeting. During 1845 he preached only three times per week. Minutes of the District Meeting of the Bechuana District, January and November 1845.

[5] This wish goes far to cast doubt on Smith's *Memoir*, p. 28.

[6] This was not acknowledged by the District Meeting. Although Appleyard had studied Xosa as yet he had not done any Bible translation with a view to printing, and it would seem that his proficiency was not recognised by his peers.

[7] Unidentified.

[8] John Norval, a Settler of 1820, launched the first pontoon on the Orange river in 1841 at the drift on his farm Dapperfontein. He and his project are commemorated in the modern Norval's Pont. See T. Gutsche *The Microcosm* p. 77.

[9] Probably Field-Cornet G. Joubert. See G. E. Cory *Rise of South Africa*, Vol. IV pp. 68–72. Joubert was active as a mediator in the Boer-Griqua disputes of 1845.

[10] Unidentified.

[11] See Introduction to Chap. II, p. 28. Campbell was in command of the detachment of 91st Regt. stationed at Colesberg.

¹² G. A. Kolbe had his connection with the London Missionary Society dissolved, by the Society, in 1837.
¹³ Rev. F. Taylor, ?–1844, died at the age of 28.
¹⁴ On 5th February 1845. There seems to have been some doubt as to whether Appleyard was to remain in the Bechuana District for another year, for he was not appointed to any post. P. Smailes, assistant missionary, was appointed to Colesberg. The Albany and Kaffraria District Meeting of 7 January 1845 appointed Appleyard to the Beka, but the move was delayed for a year.
¹⁵ There were Paris Evangelical Mission stations in Basuto country, Cape Colony and the Bechuana country: Thaba Bosiu, Mekuatling, Morija, Bethulie, Motito, Beersheba.
¹⁶ Rev. R. Giddy, 1806–1881.
¹⁷ Probably on Norval's farm Dapperfontein. The Civil Commissioner of Colesberg had no accommodation for the cavalry, T. Gutsche, *The Microcosm*, p. 85.
¹⁸ Expulsion from the Society was by no means rare.
¹⁹ Active in the Tarka area in the war of 1846–7, where he destroyed a village in error. G. E. Cory, *Rise of South Africa*, Vol. IV p. 479.
²⁰ The Second Catechism was one of a series published by order of the British Wesleyan Conference in 1823. Whereas the first Catechism applied to children of tender age, the second was for those of seven years and more. Information from Mr. J. M. Berning, Cory Library.
²¹ Shaw was present at the meeting. There is no hint in the Minutes of Appleyard's impending departure, so presumably Shaw had the matter in his personal charge.
²² This District Meeting commenced at Graham's Town on 14th January 1846. Appleyard now had Wesleyville and not the Gwanga station under his superintendence. The Beka and Wesleyville together served most of Pato's tribe. Suddenly, also, he was put in charge of the printing press. The extract from the Minutes reads: "Bro. Dugmore is removed to the important station at D'Urban, and Brother Appleyard to the Beka with charge of our printing press at Newton-Dale. It is desirable to have these two brethren near each other, & near the press; as on them will devolve the greater part of the work connected with the revision and printing of the Kaffir version of the Scriptures." Cory Library MS 15,023. The only mention which Appleyard makes of the press occurs on page 47 where he is concerned that the press and the types be taken to Fort Peddie for safe-keeping.

For the first time Appleyard is mentioned in the Minutes in connection with Biblical translation. He undertook to translate the Books of Ezra, Nehemiah and Esther.
²³ This does not agree with A. Gordon-Brown's note on p. 108 of: *Narrative of Private Buck Adams*.

Introduction to Chapter III

Appleyard arrived in the Eastern Cape again just in time to see the beginning of the War of the Axe, 1846–1847.

The Glenelg-Stockenstrom Treaty System depended on a contractual relationship between the Xosa and the Colonists. By the end of 1845 the relationship was obviously breaking up. The treaties had been modified since their inception in 1836, but to the authorities it seemed that some of the tribes no longer valued peace. A "war party" had grown up and was countenanced by the young chief Sandili, son of Gaika and recently acclaimed paramount chief of the western Xosa.

Restlessness spread among the Xosa to the extent that Captain Maclean, successor to Shepstone as Diplomatic Agent to the Gunukwebis, was told by the chief Umkye that should hostilities break out he would have no control over his tribesmen. Maclean suspected Pato of being the "chief instigator" of unrest, but this was never proved.[1]

The Colonial authorities under Governor Sir Peregrine Maitland were willing to stick to only the spirit of the treaties if, in overlooking minor infringements of the cattle-stealing variety, they could preserve peace. But in March 1846, ten days after Appleyard returned to the Beka, an incident occurred which broke both the spirit and the letter of the treaties. One of Tola's men, living close to Fort Beaufort on the frontier, was arrested for allegedly stealing an axe from a store in the village. The local magistrate sent the accused off to Graham's Town for trial in the charge of a small party of the Cape Mounted Rifles. En route the party was attacked on colonial territory by men of the accused's kraal and the accused was freed. One of the troops was killed. Neither Tola nor his superior chief Botma nor the paramount Sandili would give up the accused or the attackers. This was regarded by Col. Hare, the Lieutenant-Governor of the Eastern Cape, as demanding punishment of the chiefs involved.

It was desirable not to declare a general war. The Governor refused Lt. Gov. Hare's advice to drive Pato and others from their lands on the frontier, because there was insufficient evidence of their implication. He ordered a concentration of troops on the guilty parties in the hope that hostilities could be localised.² The colonial forces moved into Xosa territory on 11 April 1846. Perhaps if this campaign had been successful, or even prudently conducted, other tribes might have ignored Sandili's request for help. As it was the Xosa gained a signal victory in their destruction of the wagon train at Burn's Hill, and over the following three months most of the western Xosa tribes became involved.

So began another long frontier war, waged, in Maitland's words, "with a foe so numerous and active, which carries no commissariat, passes everywhere through the bush unperceived, till a sudden assault is made, and retires with a rapid dexterity, for which the civilised man is no match . . ."³

In such circumstances the local army commanders, and especially those at the exposed Fort Peddie, were not anxious to risk their men where the odds were against them.

For several months the 1,250 active regulars were on the defensive over a frontier of nearly 90 miles. Xosa strategy concentrated on cutting supply and communications lines between the outposts. Escorts had to be large, although it was still possible to avoid the Xosa bands, as the "postmen" proved.⁴ The Xosa did succeed in keeping Peddie "poor".

The military importance of the Peddie garrison was paramount in the first half of the war. Probably more Xosa warriors were killed in this neighbourhood than anywhere else in this war.⁵ The "Battle of Peddie" saw the most awe-inspiring collection of Xosa tribesmen since the Battle of Graham's Town in 1819. The famous cavalry charge which hacked down hundreds occurred on the nearby banks of the Gwanga. And there was regularly at least a skirmish when a supply train pushed its way through the Fish river bush.

Appleyard was a spectator of the Battle of Peddie, and he had first-hand accounts of many of the other engagements. He was deeply involved: some of the enemy had been in his church, and he had visited others; they destroyed his home and his books; the Fingoes who were fighting for the British were in some cases well-known to him. And yet Appleyard's care for accuracy is clear throughout. The destruction of his mission station is stated without any colourful comment.⁶ His statements and estimates of men killed and cattle taken are always critical. He corrects previous statements which he has discovered to be wrong, and he retails rumours only when he labels them. Later in the year Maitland himself had cause to animadvert on the alarmism in the frontier press which printed

A Patrol at Ease

unfounded reports and had troops hurrying off on wild goose chases.[7]

Some description of the appearance of the various British and colonial troops in the field will not be out of place. It applies largely also to the war of 1850-52 (See chapter V below). Probably the most effective way of doing this is to quote an extract from Dr. Monro's autobiography. (He was stationed at Fort Peddie during the War of the Axe as Assistant Surgeon to the 91st Regiment):

> "The cavalry – big men, well-mounted on the largest horses procurable in the colony – wore a blue forage-cap, red jacket, and blue cloth pantaloons . . . The soldier of the line, a fine, well-developed, and well-set-up man, of an average height of five feet eight inches, was clad in blue forage-cap, red jacket, and white linen trousers for the march, his dark grey cloth ones being rolled up in his great-coat for night use. The Cape Corps [Cape Mounted Rifles], little men mounted on small, active horses, wore blue forage-cap, green cloth jacket, and brown buckskin trousers, or *crackers*, as they were called. The Boer cut a curious figure, in his slouched felt hat, generally trimmed with black ostrich feathers, loose, homespun jacket and waistcoat, buckskin trousers, and veldt shun [veldskoen]. He was always on horseback, rode with a loose rein, long stirrups, and careless seat, usually on a small horse much under his weight, for he is a big, heavy fellow, as a rule. The Hottentot Levies, composed of the same style of men as the Cape Corps, were dressed in wideawake felt hats, cloth jacket, crackers, and veldt shun, with a blanket rolled over the shoulder . . . The Fingoes appeared in war-paint and blanket."[8]

The arms carried by the regulars consisted for the most part of smooth-bore muskets with flintlocks – the old "Brown Bess" – or the newer variety with percussion locks. These guns were not relied on to hit anything at a range of over 300 yards. Munro explains that the recoil from the muskets was so bad that most of the soldiers did not use the full charge of powder. The Cape Mounted Rifles was more effectively armed with a short, double-barrelled, smooth-bore carbine which excelled in irregular warfare. The Boer's "roer" Munro describes as being a "magnified blunderbuss", but very effective. The Hottentot Levies for the most part carried flintlock muskets and some of the Fingoes had muskets but they, for the most part, used shield and assegai.

Notes and References

[1] Maclean to Hare, enclosures in Maitland to Stanley, 31 March 1846, PP 786, p. 84 & 92.
[2] Maitland to Hare, 30 March 1846. Enclosure in Maitland to Stanley, ibid. p. 96.
[3] Maitland to Stanley, 24 April, 1846. ibid. p. 116.
[4] See below, p. 57 & 59.
[5] See below, Appleyard's detailed list of casualties, p. 71.
[6] See below, p. 46, 101.
[7] Maitland to Grey, 14 October 1846. Ibid. p. 198.
[8] Munro, W., *Records of Service and Campaigning in Many Lands*, Vol. I, pp. 204-7.

Chapter III

The War of the Axe (i)

March 18th : Through the kind providence of our Heavenly Father, my steps have been once more directed to the Beka, where I arrived on Friday night the 6th inst. We have received a cordial welcome from the people, who seem pleased at our return. May the Lord make me useful to them!
March 22nd : Preached this morning at Fort Peddie to the military. As I was riding up to the Post a letter was put into my hands from Rev. W. Shaw, stating that war was likely to be made immediately against the Border Kafir tribes, and that I was to remove at once to D'Urban, and likewise the other Missionaries & Catechists living on the Frontier.[1]
March 23rd : Last night we packed up our clothes and part of our books. This morning it rained so hard that we could not stir out. At mid-day it cleared up, and about that time Pato, Dilima,[2] Xosa, and some of the Amapakati[3] arrived, to know why the Traders were leaving the country, and to see what I was going to do. I told him that war was likely to take place, and that therefore I was going to remove for the present, as Missionaries had nothing to do with war. He appeared to be alarmed at the thought of the English making war, but he is such a deceitful character, that he cannot be fathomed. He came a second time alone, and said that he was not willing that we should leave, but that we must sit still. I told him, however, that the word had come from Mr. Shaw, and that I must listen to it. After he left the Station I prepared to leave myself, as I expected if we waited till the next day, we should find it difficult to do so, if he persisted in our not going. At dark accordingly we put what things we could into the Trader's wagon, and came here (D'Urban) in the night.
March 25th : Last night Mr. Kidd[4] and family arrived. This

morning Mr. Brownlee[5] of the London Society and his family arrived, and in the evening Messrs. Green[6] and Webb[7] and their families. We have quartered ourselves as well as we could on the Mission Premises. The immediate cause of the present warlike demonstration on the part of the Colonial Government, is the capture of a Kafir prisoner from the Escort, and the murder of the Hottentot who was handcuffed with him, taken in connection with the very general stealing of Colonial horses and cattle which has been going on for some time past.[8]

March 30th: Yesterday being the Sabbath I preached at the Post in the morning, and at the Station in the afternoon to the Mission families and Traders. The Fingoes also had their usual services, Mr. Brownlee officiating in the morning and Mr. Kidd at mid-day. As yet we have heard nothing certain about the intentions of the Government. Every preparation, however, is making for the adoption of the most vigorous measures. With regard to the Kafirs it is difficult to form an opinion. Doubtless many are ready to avail themselves of the opportunity for plunder which war would afford them. On the other hand, several of the chiefs appear to deprecate war, but their influence for good is very little, and consequently no dependence can be placed on their mere profession of friendship. My whole dependence is upon God. May He sit at the helm of affairs, and render all circumstances subservient to the furtherance of His cause in this dark and benighted land!

April 1st: By the post of last night, I received a letter from Mr. Shaw stating that war was decided upon in Cape Town, and that an express had gone out to the Country districts to call out the Burgher force.[9] We may expect war, therefore, to commence in a few days. Still we have no intelligence of what the government intend to do; whether the attack is to be upon the whole of the Border tribes, or upon the Amagqeka[10] (sic) alone. This morning intelligence arrived of the death of the old Chief Qeno.[11] Since the last war he has been perhaps the most faithful of all the Kafir chiefs to the British government.

April 2nd : Pato and Kobi were here to-day. It appears that our Beka has been entered and some of the windows broken. The man, however, is known, and Pato has his eye upon him for future settlement.

April 3rd : Last night I received another letter from Mr. Shaw, containing a message from him to Umhala and Pato. The latter came this afternoon and I delivered it to him, and impressed upon him the necessity of himself and his people sitting still. The Lieut. Governor has proclaimed war against Sandili, Maqomo,[12] Botman and Tola,[13] and ordered the Burgher force to be in readiness to act with the Military. He has also sent friendly messages to Umhala, Umkye, and Stock.[14] Pato is not noticed except in a private communication, and there he is spoken of unfavourably. The Government are evidently very suspicious of him, but if he observes a complete neutrality, I believe they will let him alone.

April 5th : Preached on the Post at 3 o'clock. Received another message from Mr. Shaw to Pato, warning him of danger, and telling him to beware.

April 8th : No particular intelligence arrived by the post. The Governor is daily expected in Graham's Town.

April 10th : Being Good Friday, I preached at Major Yarborough's[15] request to some of the Troops this afternoon.

April 11th : Last night an express arrived from Fort Beaufort, bringing information that an attack was to be made upon Botman's kraal at day light this morning. This, I suppose, would be the commencement of the war.[16]

Saw Col. Lindsay[17] who requested to have the Sacrament of the Lord's supper administered during the approaching Sabbath. He informed me also that he was going with a patrole to Pato's place, to see what he was about, and also, I believe, to deliver some message to him, at dawn to-morrow.

April 12th : A very wet and cold day. I held service with the

Fingoes and baptized a son of Simka.[18] Mr. Brownlee preached to us in English in the afternoon. Prevented by the weather from administering the Sacrament as was intended. Col. Lindsay's visit to Pato appears to have been a very foolish and ill-advised affair. As might have been expected the first appearance of the troops drove all into the bush, and Pato was not to be seen.[19]

April 15th : Pato came last night after a great deal of persuasion. He had an interview with Capt. Maclean[20] to-day, which appears to have restored his confidence. Very little intelligence of the operations of the troops by the post. We have heard, however, that the Gaikas have fled over the Keiskamma with all their cattle.

April 19th : Preached at the Post this morning, and here in the afternoon. After the latter service I administered the Sacrament to the members of the church, both English and natives.

April 20th : Intelligence has arrived that 2,000 head of cattle have been taken from the Kafirs after two days hard fighting. In retreating with them to Block drift, however, the baggage wagons, which appear to have been left to follow on without sufficient protection, were plundered and burnt, and all the oxen captured.[21] The Kafirs then proceeded on and fell on the troops, but were eventually repulsed. Up to this time the loss in killed and wounded, is about 30 on the English side, and about 200 on the Kafir side.[22] One of the Dragoon Captains is killed,[23] and another of the 91st is wounded. It is said that the troops march again to-day from Block Drift.

April 21st : We were suddenly alarmed this morning by the intelligence that the Kafirs were coming upon us. We immediately removed to Fort Peddie, where a room[24] was provided for us by Mr. Castray of the Commissariat, and where Mr. Green was also staying. We sent over a few things by hand, thankful that we were so near a place of refuge. The Kafirs however did not attack us, and we afterwards found out that they are only at present assembling themselves together at the Keiskamma river. We spent the night at the Infantry Barracks.[25]

April 22nd: No news of the Kafirs except that they are still assembling and moving nearer to us, with the intention of attacking the Post. Pato has not made his appearance this morning as we desired. I fear he will prove unfaithful to the Government. The women and children slept at the Barracks.

Bro. Green, myself and others staid at Mr. Castray's, keeping watch most of the night, being apprehensive of a sudden attack from the Kafirs.

April 23rd: All quiet till mid-day, when we were alarmed by the war-cry and the Fingoes bringing in their cattle in great haste. The troops were all ordered out in readiness for action, whilst a small party went out to reconnoitre. Soon after an express came in stating that the Fingoes were engaged with some of Pato's Kafirs, who were endeavouring to make off with the cattle of Jokwini's[26] people. The Dragoons and a gun were immediately started off, but they were too late to be of any service, the Fingoes, assisted by the small party first sent off, having retaken their cattle and driven the Kafirs away.

The post arrived this morning, but only brought intelligence to the 10th. inst. The escort stated the Fish river bush was full of Kafirs, so that we are now pretty well surrounded by enemies. But "if God be for us, who can be against us." In Him is our defence.

April 24th: Nothing particular has occurred to-day, though the Kafirs still surround us.

April 25th: Mr. Cumming[27] of the Glasgow African society arrived to-day from his station at the Igqibira. An alarm was given at mid-day, and the cattle were seen coming in from Pato's side of the settlement. A small party went out, and found that the Fingoes had seen two Kafir spies, one of whom was Matyumzi,[28] and also about thirty Kafirs in two parties, apparently watching an opportunity to carry off cattle. About 150 Kafirs were also seen through the glass, to be assembled at Xosa's place. In the afternoon Um-Kai sent for Mr. Tainton to learn the truth or falsehood of some report which had been carried to him, to the effect that the troops were intending to fall upon him, as well as to give some information in reference to the Kafirs. He advised us not to sleep to-night, as he had heard that Umhala was to join Pato in an attack upon the post. Umhala's people, however, had not reached the place of meeting, but Umkai (sic) had sent off messengers to his brother[29] to learn whether what he had heard was true, and promised to send news as soon as they returned. Pato appears to have involved himself, though Saba, one of Stock's brothers, said on Friday last in Mr. Cumming's hearing, that Stock and Pato were going to sit still. He refuses to come here although Maclean has sent for him twice.

April 26th: A beautiful day which we were permitted to enjoy undisturbed. We had all our services on the Post. Mr. Brownlee preached to the troops in the morning, and I in the afternoon. Mr. Kidd preached to the Hottentots, Mr. Tainton[30] to the Fingoes, and Mr. Cumming to the English civilians.

Last night the Fingoes chased about 30 of Pato's Kafirs almost to Pato's kraal. One of them was stabbed. The Fingoes observed them prowling about, and on their not being able to give the password at once attacked them.

In the afternoon Um-Qai sent in a messenger to hear the news, and to tell us that his messenger had not arrived from Umhala. He also said that though we had no attack last night, we were not to be careless, but watch all night.

April 27th: Heard some intelligence about the operations of the troops at Block Drift from some of Stock's Kafirs. They relate that the Kafirs surrounded the place, expecting to starve the troops, and then get the ammunition. In ignorance of British skill they got into a blind river within reach of the guns in considerable numbers. Here many were killed, and it is said that our troops had to go over their dead bodies in order to pursue those who endeavoured to escape.[31] It is

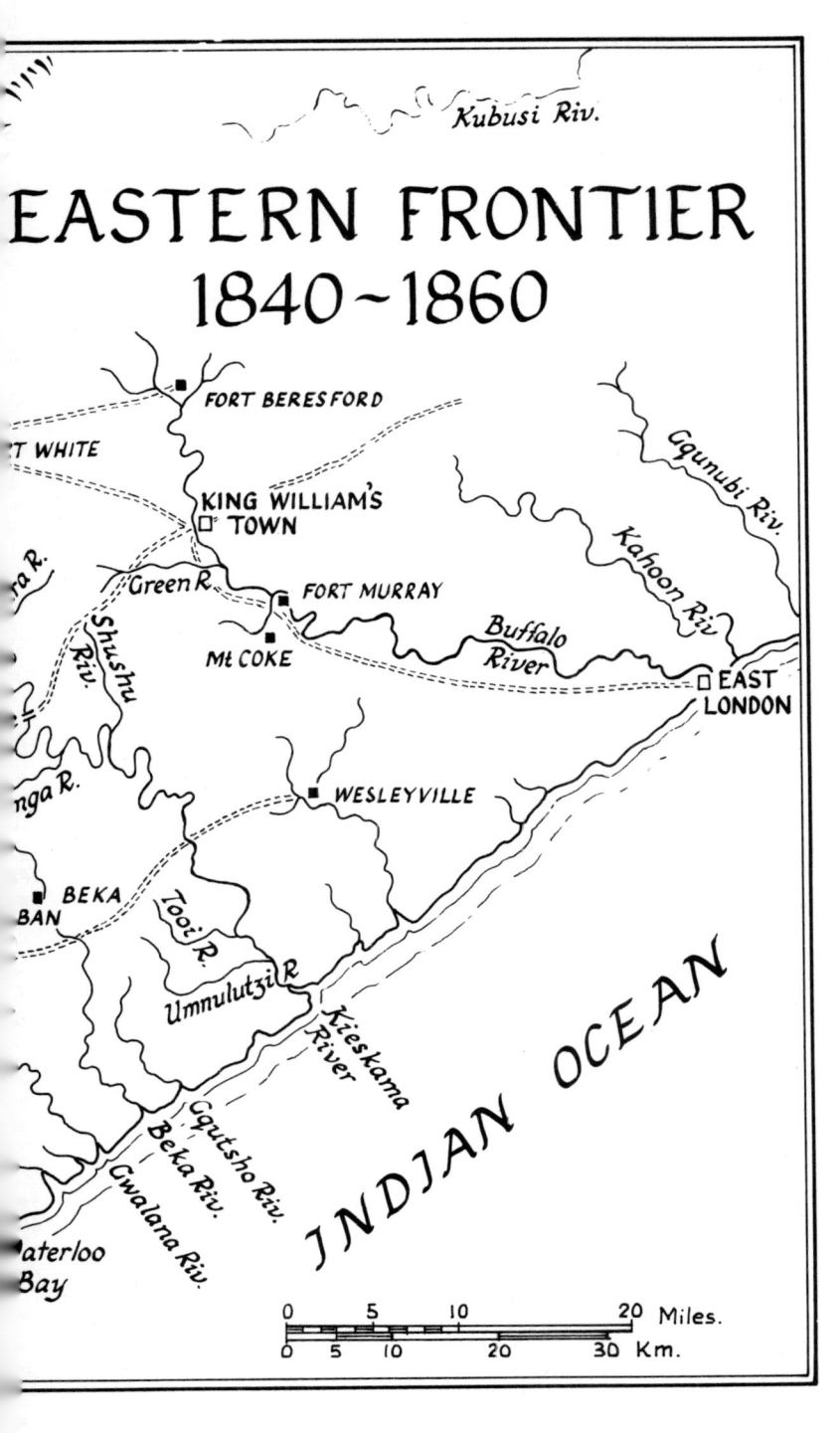

doubtless this information which has paralyzed the Kafirs in this part, and prevented them from making their intended attack. It is reported also that they could not agree among themselves as to the system of attack, and that some have returned home, whilst a few have gone into the colony.[32] Thus the Lord shows us that He reigneth. We are still, however, in a state of great anxiety, more especially at night.

Reports have also reached us of attacks upon some of the Frontier posts. Some Kafirs in returning from that made upon Fort Brown[33] are represented as having told Um-Qai or some of his people, that they found the work too hard. I believe about 30 of them had been killed, whilst their booty was only a few oxen. It is said that Tola and his Kafirs are gone into the colony, with the intention of proceeding into Lower Albany. Some of Siyolo's[34] Kafirs are also reported to have gone into the Colony, whilst others with Siyolo himself have returned home. I heard this morning, too, that a few of Pato's people had moved into the Colony.

April 28th: All has been quiet to-day. Last night most of the females remained at home.

April 29th: Heard this morning that Pato had sent to Stock to join the war. He replied that he was sitting upon his fathers grave.[35] He said also in reference to Fort Peddie, that it would be a national disgrace to attack it, as there were several women and children and Missionaries there.

Several bodies of Kafirs have passed into the Colony. The tracks of some have been seen by the Fingoe scouts. Vast herds of cattle have been stolen and brought into Kafirland. This afternoon Col. Richardson arrived with 4 troops of the Dragoons and 1 troop of the Cape Corps from Post Victoria.[36] They state that they have had hard work with the Kafirs. The loss on the side of the troops is 16 killed and several wounded. On the side of the Kafirs three or four hundred at least have been killed. The Kafirs have all left Block Drift and its neighbourhood, and, it is supposed are gone into the colony. We have doleful intelligence from the vicinity of Fort

Beaufort.³⁷ The Kafirs have burnt several houses and swept almost all before them. Several civilians are reported to have been killed. We hear also that the Mission premises at Burn's hill are destroyed, except the church, Sandili saying that he did not fight against that, but against the people.

Umhala's message³⁸ to Umkye was heard to-day. It was to the effect that he was engaged at present in marrying another wife.

April 30th : This forenoon we were again alarmed by the war cry. It arose from three different quarters of the Settlement at about the same time. The principal cause was an attack of a large party of Pato's Kafirs, who succeeded in getting off with six herds of cattle, including all mine,³⁹ and a flock of goats.

The Fingoes attacked the Kafirs, who were greatly superior to them, in point of numbers, and succeeded in driving them back to the Beka. The troops, after a most unaccountable delay of two or three hours,⁴⁰ marched to the help of the Fingoes, and with the intention of attacking Xosa's place, but did nothing beyond firing a few shells into the bush, and then retreating to the Post, as they found the Kafirs more numerous than they anticipated. Four Fingoes were killed, and amongst these was Umboni, a resident of our D'Urban station, and formerly a servant of mine. Two Kafirs were also killed, but it is not known whether any were killed by the shells in the bush. Soon after the troops had gone, we perceived smoke arising in the direction of the Beka. Bro. Green and myself immediately started on horseback to the point from which we could see our Mission premises, and on arriving at the spot our worst fears were confirmed. The trader's establishment, the people's houses, and the church appeared to be all burning. About the Mission house we could not be certain, as it had not a thatch roof, but a flat one covered with paper. This evening a strong light was for some time visible in the direction of Newtondale, and we fear therefore that our Mission premises there are also destroyed. Pato has now shown himself in his true colours, and we can no longer doubt his intentions. I scarcely thought that he would proceed so far as to burn our stations, after so many years of Missionary labour in his country, and after such loud and continued professions of good-will. The women and children have again gone to the Barracks, in case we should have a night attack. May the Lord preserve them and us, and sanctify these painful events to our present and everlasting good!

May 1st : This day has passed over quietly through the kind providence of our heavenly Father. Bro. Green and myself rode to the top of the hill, and examined the Beka station through a telescope. We could see the destruction of all but the Mission house, which appeared to be yet whole unless they have done mischief inside. Afterwards we assisted in getting over our printing press and types,[41] which, for want of better accomodation, we have put under Mr. Castray's verandah.

A report came in this afternoon that the Kafirs were assembled near the Gwalana, whither they probably removed, expecting the troops would have gone out this morning in the direction of the Beka. Fingoe spies are out to watch their movements. Umkye was here to-day, and brings us the intelligence that Umhala was still sitting still, and that he intended to eat up all of his people that joined the war party.

May 2nd : The Kafirs are again around us. Pato's people are at the old Gwalana post, and we learn through Umkye that many of Umhala's people, as well as Nonibi's[42] and Siyolo's, and even some of Sandili's, are this side of the Keiskamma. Pato considers the retreat of the troops as a defeat,[43] and has sent a ludicrous account of what he considers his victory to Stock, again inviting him to join him in the war. Stock, however, ordered his messengers off, telling them they were to bring no more war news to his children. A small party of Kafirs were seen by the Fingoes this evening, on some ploughed land about two miles from the Post, and others were coming out of the bush. A party of Fingoes have gone out to watch their movements.

The war-cry was again heard this morning. Four mounted Kafirs were observed approaching the Fingoe cattle, and it was supposed that these only formed the advanced guard of the enemy. After firing, however, two or three shots they retired.

Col. Lindsay issued "garrison orders" this evening, to inform the women and children, that they were not to go to the Barracks unless there was real danger, and the men capable of bearing arms, that they were to defend their own dwellings in case of attack.

May 3rd: We were only able to have our morning services to-day, the others being prevented by the report of Kafirs in the immediate neighbourhood. The troops went out with two guns in the direction of the Gwanga, but returned without accomplishing any thing, the Kafirs running away as soon as they made their appearance, after firing our Mission premises at the Gwanga, and which were seen in flames from the Tower.[44] Four Burghers arrived in the morning from Trumpetter's[45] with papers and letters from Graham's Town, up to the 28th ultimate.

May 4th: Heard this morning that about 20 Kafirs were killed by the shell-firing last Thursday, and that a chief was wounded. Also that Stock had divided his men into two commandoes, to keep the frontier line from Umkye's country to about Fort Wiltshire, and to intercept all cattle stolen from the Colony. It is said that Pato has sent word to the Kafirs who surround us, that they are not to fight till Xasana[46] arrives. A post from Fort Beaufort arrived this morning, bringing doleful intelligence from that part. Large quantities of cattle have been taken, many sheep destroyed, and some lives lost. Commissariat supplies also arrived safely from Graham's Town. A few letters and papers were received. Col. Somerset had arrived in that part, much to the relief of the Graham's Town people, who appear to have sustained something like a siege for a week previously.[47] His Excellency has proclaimed Martial law,[48] and assumed the command of the troops. His Honour, it is supposed, will now have to take the field. Our troops here remain still, much to the surprize of many. The Fingoes have had all the fighting hitherto to themselves.

May 5th : A report came in before day-light that a large herd of cattle were passing, having been stolen from the colony. A few troops went out in pursuit, after a delay of some time, and of course saw nothing but their spoer, the Kafirs having had plenty of time to cross the Keiskamma before they could have come up with them. The spoer of Kafirs going into the colony was also seen. A few Kafirs were detected last night trying to get off some horses from one of the outside kraals.[49] The Fingoes drove them off, but the Kafirs told them that it would make no difference, as they were coming back in the morning. They have not put their threat into execution, however, though the Fingoes, to the number of 50 or 60, assembled on the post in full expectation of their attack. It is confidently reported that Pato's son, Mati, has been killed in the vicinity of Bathurst.[50]

May 6th : Very early this morning a strong party of Fingoes, about 150 in number, went out with a few of the Cape Corps for the purpose of capturing any cattle which they might find coming from the colony. They took the direction of Newtondale, keeping rather close to the Fish river bush. Soon after sun-rise they succeeded in bringing off upwards of 500 head of cattle and 3 horses, belonging to Lama's[51] people, the very chief who attacked Jokwini's tribe some days since. They brought them some distance without much resistance on the part of the Kafirs, but as they began to make for the Post, the Kafirs were seen approaching in considerable numbers. Two of the Cape Corps were then dispatched hither, and soon afterwards some more of the Cape Corps, and a troop of the 7th Dragoons, who had had their horses saddled since 5 o'clock, went to their succour, taking also some of the Artillery and a gun. On the appearance of this reinforcement the Kafirs fled, and all the cattle were brought in with no loss on our part, whilst of the Kafirs 5 had been killed and two or three wounded. On inquiring I found that our Mission premises at Newtondale had not been burnt, but only the trader's place, and, I believe, some forage.

Scarcely had the captured cattle been got safely on the Post, before smoke was seen ascending in the direction where some commissariat wagons were loading up wood. In a short time the conductor, R. Tainton Junr.,[52] was seen galloping towards the Post. On arriving he stated that the Kafirs had succeeded in capturing the oxen of the hindmost wagon, and were proceeding in their attack on the next. A party of the 7th Dragoons were immediately sent to their succour, whilst another party with a gun went in another direction to try and intercept the Kafirs should they fly. A span of oxen was also sent to replace those which had been taken, and shortly afterwards the wagons arrived, when it was found that the tent of the last one was burnt, and that it was a good deal injured in other parts from attempts to get it on fire. The Kafirs who attacked the wagons were all mounted and the small escort of about 20 men had sharp work to defend themselves. One Kafir was killed and another wounded, but there were no casualties on our side, though there were some hairbreadth escapes. R. Tainton was most providentially preserved, as he was fired at two or three times. On the Dragoons coming up to the wagons, the Kafirs fled with great precipitancy. The Dragoons gave them chase, however, at full gallop, and pursued them for a considerable distance, but were obliged to pull in a little beyond our Gwanga station and commence their retreat, as they saw not far before them between one and two thousand Kafirs.

Umkye came in this evening with his cattle and family.[53] Some of his cattle also have been stolen by the Kafirs. He advises no one to sleep to-night, as he thinks it very likely that there will be an attack. The Colonel nevertheless refuses permission for the women and children to sleep at the Barracks, but promises that they shall have due warning given them, at which time they may go there.

May 7th: No attack from the Kafirs, as anticipated, last night, but they have moved nearer to us, having been discovered by the Fingoe scouts in a ravine about two or three miles from the Post. The Post came in this morning from Graham's Town, bringing us intelligence up to the 5th instant. His Excellency is now in Graham's Town, and Col. Richardson's party is to proceed to Bathurst. The most remarkable feature of the present warfare, is the wonderful preservation of life on the side of the Colonists. Though there has been a vast loss in the way of property, yet the loss of life has been very small. This can be only ascribed to a miraculous interposition of Divine Providence, and as such all Christians should acknowledge it.

The Kafirs are already beginning to mourn. They have lost many of their petty chiefs and great men in the colony. The Imi-Dushani,[54] especially, are said to have suffered greatly.

The captured cattle were divided out to the Fingoes who were in yesterday's expedition. Six were given to the soldiers for slaughter, and a span of oxen and a horse to the European guide.

Martial law was proclaimed here to-day, as it had been before in the Colony.

May 8th: A few Kafirs were bold enough to come out of the bush last evening, and were seen at Fani's kraal,[55] which is within sight of the Post. They were not meddled with, however, by the Authorities here, any further than that spies were appointed to watch them. Fani had run away the previous night, and the Fingoes brought away his kraal[56] to-day. This morning Col. Richardson's party left us en route to Bathurst, where it is to be hoped they will be more active and useful than they have been here. They had some skirmishing with the Kafirs in the road. It appeared as if the advanced party, who were in charge of 4 wagons, had been attacked, as one or two men were seen riding back to hasten the remainder on. On Mr. Shepstone[57] and others going out to see whether anything had happened, they heard the war-cry sounding through the Fish river bush, and also the firing of artillery. From the dust, however, they judged that the troops were near the Brack river,[58] and had passed the Kafirs. Two messengers arrived from Umhala, having spent the night at Umkye's place. The news they bring is cheering. Umhala is still sitting still and intends to continue so. He says, moreover, that he shall treat any of his people who join the war against the English as thieves. Xasana,[59] who arrived two or three days since, has been ordered home, and report says, that Pato is now left with only his body guard, most of his people being in the Colony. Mati's[60] death is confirmed, having been shot as he was driving a Fatherland[61] cow. Pafa, another of Pato's sons was badly wounded. It seems pretty clear that Umhala has been playing a deep game. He has got Pato fairly involved in the war, without committing himself personally, and now leaves him to his fate. Hayi! ubulumko bukam. Bodhla, asi nokuba bu kulu.[62]

A Fingoe girl, the daughter of one of Jokwini's people living in Pato's country, ran away to this Settlement last night under the most distressing circumstances. It appears that Pato has issued an order that all the Fingoes in his country are to be killed, to prevent them from going over to the side of Government, and thus strengthen their hands.[63] The father of this girl was accordingly killed, and horrible to relate, her mother was burnt alive in the hut. Surely the vengeance of Heaven will descend upon the wretched man who is the author of such atrocities. It is justly to be feared that the blood of many rests on his guilty head. No wonder, therefore, if the Lord, "the righteous Judge", should at length give him up to certain destruction.

May 9th: Heard that Lama[64] was amongst the 5 or 6 Kafirs who were killed last Wednesday. Also the particulars of the

Burghers from Cape Town

death of the Fingoe, and which vary somewhat from the report which I heard yesterday, and recorded above. It appears that Pato issued an order, the same day that he attacked the Settlement and burnt our Beka station, to the effect that all Fingoes living in his country, as well as Kafirs who were known to be friendly to the Government, should be killed. How many may have fallen victims to this bloody law time alone can reveal. One case, however, has come to light. The same night that the Beka station was destroyed, some Kafirs surrounded the hut of a Fingoe living on the Gqutsho.[65] The man went out to see what was the matter, when he was instantly assassinated. A woman, who was following him, was struck by assegais and fell dead at the door as she was going out. There were yet in the hut a woman and a lad of about 16, and perhaps others, and on these not coming out, the Kafirs blocked up the door and deliberately set fire to the hut, with the intention of burning them alive. Yesterday this woman and boy arrived on the settlement, having been 8 or 9 days getting here, and without food except roots and water, all the time. Their state is truly painful to behold, and it is wonderful however they managed to get here. Capt. Maclean has kindly interfered on their behalf, and provided them with lodging and surgical assistance.

The Kafirs are beginning to be tired of going into the colony. Some who have returned say they shall not go again, they have had so many narrow escapes. Several of Pato's people, it is said, who returned wounded, have since died, and this is doubtless the case with other tribes.

I forgot to record before that, at the time when Sandili made such a demonstration before his Honour, I believe, at Block drift, a most remarkable interposition of Divine Providence took place. It appears that a man was appointed by Sandili, to watch for the most favourable opportunity in which the Troops might be fallen upon, and to give the signal of attack by the firing of a gun. It has since come out privately, that this man made three several attempts to fire off the gun, but he failed in every instance, and then gave up. It was the intention of the Kafirs on that occasion to murder every soul. This shows that the Kafirs have long intended war, and were only waiting a favourable opportunity to commence it. There is a rumour that Kobi[66] is anxious to keep out of the war, but Pato threatens to destroy him should he make any attempt to leave his country.

May 10th: A quiet Sabbath. We held all our services. I preached to the troops in the afternoon.

May 11th: Nothing stirring to-day. Most of the Kafirs appear to have gone off to the Colony. Smoke seen in the distance, and in various directions, this and the two or three previous days. Supposed to arise principally from the burning of grass. Six families of Fingoes are said to have perished in consequence of Pato's edict, so far as we have yet been able to learn. Umkye had an interview with Maclean to-day, and, in reference to the murder of Mr. Scholtz,[67] asked how it was that the English were so blind. Pato, said he, had a hand in that murder, though a missionary was not intended to be the victim.

May 12th: Post from Graham's Town by Kafir Jack.[68] Some sharp remarks upon the Beka affair in the "Journal",[69] but substantially true.

A slight affair between the Fingoes and some Kafirs. The latter were trying to get off with some cattle, when the war-cry was sounded as usual. The Fingoes succeeded in retaking them, though not without loss, one being killed, who was Uman-yanda's[70] head man, and another wounded.

Umkye is very sore on account of the suspicions which are entertained against him. He says, that he informed the Government from the first of the hostile state of affairs; that he has warned them of the several commandoes which have surrounded us; that he has told of his own people joining the war party, and given them over to be dealt with as they deserve; and asks if this is the manner of an enemy.

An escort of 20 men went off with Dr. Macgregor[71] for

Trumpetters drift. It appears that about 10 of the Dragoons were wounded at the Brack river⁷² last Friday. The Kafirs who attacked them were Lama's⁷³ people, and the names of two of them who were killed are known. About 10 were killed in all. A few parties of Kafirs have returned from the Colony without any booty. It is said that they found the work too hot for them, each party having lost men, varying from 5 to about 15 in number.

May 13th: The Escort returned safely from Trumpetter's this morning. They saw the dead body of a stout Kafir lying in the road, different portions of which were bespattered with blood, particularly at the top of the Fish river bush, which shows that several of the Kafirs must have been wounded. The Dragoons were engaged with the enemy about 3 hours.⁷⁴ Three of them were wounded rather badly, and remained at Trumpetters, whilst the remaining 7 were able to proceed to Town.⁷⁵ Two horses, also, were killed, and 10 wounded. There were some of Pato's people engaged as well as Lama's. One of those who were killed is Umye, one of Pato's people living near the lime kiln.⁷⁶

It has been found out that Siyolo headed the attack on the wood wagons the 6th. inst., and that they were his men who fired upon Umkye.⁷⁷ In his flight from the Dragoons Siyolo's horse knocked up, and would have found it difficult to escape, if the Dragoons had continued the chase. The Kafirs were so hard pressed that they had actually abandoned the oxen. These were cut from the wagon by a son of Umpehla,⁷⁸ who resides near the Tamara.⁷⁹

It is rumoured that people are assembling at Nonibi's, to consider what should be done with Siyolo for firing at Umkye. Also that Stock is collecting his people to attack Nonibi.⁸⁰

There are a number of Kafirs still assembled at a place called Paradise,⁸¹ almost close to the Post.

The poor Fingoe boy who was burnt out of Pato's country, died yesterday in great agony. The woman is likely to recover. Umgai, acting under the advice of Capt. Maclean, now lives on the Post, and is allowed rations for himself and 2 followers.

May 14th: Nothing of any interest has occurred to-day. Heard a rumour that Sonto, having obtained a pretty good booty, now intends to join his brother Stock.[82]

May 15th: Pato has sent a message to Sandili that he is fast about attacking this Post. One thing which hinders him is that Umkye is here.[83]

The Gaikas, it is said, have now nearly all returned from the Colony. Maqomo is in the Amatola mountains, and Sandili somewhere in the neighbourhood. The Kafirs who are still about are mostly Pato's and Nonibi's. There is a Kafir rumour that the Officer at Block drift[84] has sent to Sandili, to ask what he is about that he does not sue for peace. This of course must be a fabrication.

Some wagons went out again yesterday for wood, but they were not molested, though nearly a hundred Kafirs were seen sitting at the edge of the bush, as if warming themselves in the sun.

Fani[85] who ran away from the Settlement the other day went to Stock's, and afterwards to Umkye's. Umkye however, was not at home, and Fani only met with him to-day. He told Umkye that he had been obliged to run away, but was sorry that he had done so without telling Maclean. Umkye told him that the best proof he could give of his friendly disposition to the Government, would be to go and see what Pato was about, and also what Kobi was doing, and then to bring him word, and he would speak for him to Maclean. To this Fani appeared agreeable, and I believe had set out on his errand. Umgai returned to his kraal to-day, Maclean not being willing to take the responsibility of his living here, unless he would stay on the Post altogether, and to this Umgai demurred. He can still visit the Post, however, whenever he has any information to communicate, but his stay must be short.

May 16th: Nothing particular has occurred to-day.

May 17th: As I was preaching this morning, the war-cry was sounded, which compelled me to conclude as quickly as I could. Nearly all the troops turned out on this occasion, and in pretty good time. A few Kafirs were seen in the bush, and the Fingoes gave them good chase, which prevented the gun from playing upon them, as it otherwise would have done. A Kafir fired at a Fingoe, the ball going through his shield. It was this, in fact, which gave rise to the war-cry. The Kafirs, who were probably a small party returning from the Colony, effected their escape, but took no booty.

Fifteen Fingoes went down to Newtondale last evening, to see how things were looking about their old places, going, however, of their own accord. On approaching Jokwini's old kraal they discovered a small party of Kafirs, sitting round a fire. As they were more numerous than themselves, they agreed upon certain signals for firing simultaneously upon them, and then running away. This they accordingly did. How many they killed and wounded they cannot say, as they only staid long enough after firing to hear their cries. On their return they were fired upon by two different parties of Kafirs, and one poor fellow who knocked up, is supposed to have been killed.

May 18th: Umgai has come on the Post again. He has made up his mind to live here altogether. The reason of this determination arises from a message which he has heard Sandili has sent to Umhala. The substance of this message is, that as Umgai stood with the Government during the last war, and is again standing with them during this, he must be put out of the way. How Umhala will treat this message remains to be seen: but Umgai is evidently in doubt of him, and hence is (sic) present movement to be on the safe side.

Kafir Jack refuses to take the Post to Graham's Town again. He feels that the risk is too great.

May 19th: On further inquiry I find that the particulars I recorded yesterday are not exactly correct. It appears that the message of Sandili to Umhala was, not that Umgai was to be killed, but that he was to be destroyed as a chief.[86] Umgai has also heard that Umhala sent word back, that this could not be. They were children of the same man, and how could a man be deprived of his chieftainship, &c.

Umgai has not yet fully retired from his kraal. And Kafir Jack has been prevailed upon to take the post. He started this evening soon after sun-set.

Fani returned yesterday to Umgai, but is afraid to come on the Post. He says that Kobi has been compelled, at the peril of his life, to join Pato in the war. Pato also required him to scatter Webb's cattle as a proof of his doing[87] so.

Umgai has advised Maclean to apply for more troops, as Pato is still intending to attack the Post, joined by the Gaikas and the Imidushani. He has sent a message to urge Sandili on, before any more troops arrive. The plan is for the Gaikas and Imidushani to commence the attack, by taking the Fingoe cattle, as soon as they have gone out, in the direction of Mt. Somerset,[88] in order to draw the troops out some distance from the place, and then Pato will be ready to pounce upon the Post and tread it down at once.[89]

May 20th: Learnt from one of Umgai's men that the Kafirs after whom the troops turned out on Sunday last,[90] were a small party of Rili's[91] people returning from the colony with a booty of goats and cattle. Also that messengers from Umhala were on their way to Peddie. There is a Kafir rumour that the Boers have told the Tembookies to move aside that they may have a path into Kafirland. On their asking the why and the wherefore, as they were sitting still, the Boers returned for answer in effect, that a path they must and would have, whether they moved or not.[92]

The Post came in this evening from Town, being brought from the wagons at Trumpetter's by an escort of Burghers and Dragoons. The intelligence is still of a mournful cast. The colonists continue to be pillaged by the Kafirs, and it is likely that some time will elapse before the colony is sufficiently cleared to enable the troops and burgher force to enter

Kafirland.⁹³ In the midst of all, it is a matter of great thankfulness, that the hand of a gracious Providence is stretched out to save the lives of our people.

May 21st : Stock and a few of his men visited the Post to-day. Their business was of little importance. An escort of 60 or 70 men of the 91st and 4 of the Cape Corps left at 4 o'clock this morning, in order to meet the wagons which were to leave Trumpetter's on their way hither. A good deal of anxiety was felt about them, especially when they did not make their appearance as soon as might be expected. R. Tainton Junr went out with two or three others a short distance from the Post, and returned with the melancholy intelligence, that as far as he was able to discern, the wagons appeared to be on fire in the Fish river bush.⁹⁴ In about 10 minutes a party of the 7th Dragoons started for the wagons and were closely followed by the gun and the remaining Dragoons. Soon after dark, however, they returned, without having been able to accomplish any thing, it being too late to penetrate through the bush. Some civilians accompanied the troops, and brought back a most heart-rending account of the state of affairs. The road was fairly blocked up with the carcases of horses and oxen which had been shot. The wagons were in flames or hidden in volumes of smoke, and a great number of goods was lying scattered about. Worse than all two or three dead bodies were found, and amongst them that of a young man of the name of Davis,⁹⁵ who only left here last night for the purpose of seeing after Webb's wagons.⁹⁶ Every thing had the appearance of their (sic) having been a desperate affray between the escort and the Kafirs. As the Dragoons were going along, a large number of Kafirs were seen in the distance, apparently clothed in new white blankets, driving the oxen, as supposed, belonging to the wagons, in two troops towards the Gwalana, and where they will probably spend the night. They are doubtless Pato's Kafirs.

May 22nd : Kafir Jack arrived with the post. Brings intelligence that the troops had been obliged to abandon the wagons, but the letters contain few particulars of the engagement. Umgai's son came in this evening, and brings the news that Pato is flushed with his victory, and intends to attack the Post to-night or to-morrow morning. He says they have captured the wagons, and driven the troops back to Trumpetter's, and that he is determined they shall not return.

Some Fingoe spies brought in a report that a large body of Kafirs were at the Line drift of the Keiskamma. They were again sent out to watch their movements. It is supposed that most of them are Umhala's people, and that he has determined to join the war party.

May 23rd: The Escort returned from Trumpetter's, and were accompanied by two more companies of the 91st., and which we regard as a very reasonable reinforcement. One company has been accomodated in the Station chapel,[97] whilst two officers occupy a portion of the Mission house, and Harvey's[98] old house serves as a Guard room and cook house. We have not been able to gather a very clear account of the wagon affair, but enough is known to show that all was not as it should have been. The march this morning was not without disgrace, most of the Cape Corps having come in drunk. It is said also that Capt. Barney[99] was in a state of intoxication almost all the way from Post Victoria. A large body of Kafirs was seen in the bush by the Escort. Umgai is anxious to sleep in a secure place at nights, as he is in fear for his life. It is said that the Kafirs are determined to take his life if possible.

There are several bodies of Kafirs now in our immediate neighbourhood, and in almost every direction. They belong to almost every tribe in Kafirland. Were it not that the Lord is on our side, we might well despair, for "vain is our help in man."

May 24th: One of Umgai's men came in last night with the information that the Kafirs had decided upon attacking this Post either to-day or to-morrow. They are assembled around us in vast numbers, the whole strength of Kafirland being apparently bent on our destruction. In the afternoon some of Umgai's cattle and horses were brought in by part of his family. They informed us that the attack was to be made either to-night or to-morrow for certain. Being the Sabbath we had our services as usual, but in a very perturbed state of mind. It has been a day of intense anxiety. A good deal of preparation has been going on, in order to give the enemy a warm reception.

Col. Lindsay has had the Oat-hay store[100] given up, as far as possible, for the women and children, and to commence sleeping there to-night.

May 25th: Several fires were visible after dark last evening, and during the night. One was in the direction of Wesleyville. Soon after mid-night a cold and boisterous wind arose, and which has continued to the present time. In all probability this has been an instrument in the hands of a "prayer-hearing and prayer-answering God," of deterring the Kafirs from their intended attack. They must have felt the effects of the piercing cold very bitterly. At all events they have not been seen to-day, nor are they at the Gwanga, where they were known to be last evening. Truly the Lord fighteth for us.

Stock has sent in to Umgai to say, that he has been compelled to join the war-party in order to save his life, but that his heart is still right.

The Kafir commandoes received orders that they were not to look upon Umgai's place as a Chief's place, nor upon his cattle as a chiefs cattle, but to treat them as though they were a common man's and an enemy's.[101]

Piet Appel tower[102] was burnt yesterday by the Kafirs.

May 26th: This morning one of the wagon drivers, an Englishman of the name of Smith,[103] was flogged by order of Col. Lindsay, for refusing to go and cut wood for the use of the troops. He received twenty-five lashes on the bare back, and was then taken to the Hospital to be healed. This circumstance has created a good deal of unpleasant feeling against the Colonel, especially as the young man was willing to go at last, and one of his comrades fell down on his knees to implore forgiveness for him.[104]

The Board of Relief for distressed Fingoes[105] met to-day for the purpose of seeing the applicants, and hearing their cases.

We have received no intelligence about the Kafirs, though they are supposed to be still in the neighbourhood. The Fingoe spies saw some close at hand this evening.

Post from Graham's Town came in soon after dark. We are to have immediate reinforcements. Some wagons are reported to have reached the Post at Trumpetter's with supplies. Capt. C. Campbell is to go under arrest to Town, to be tried by a Court Martial for abandoning the wagons on last Thursday.[106]

May 27th: Some wagons went out this morning to fetch wood and straw. Kafirs were seen as usual, but they offered no molestation. In the afternoon, however, some of them managed to get off with a span of Sterk's[107] oxen, and a report was brought in about the same time, that a large body of Kafirs were close at hand, and apparently coming on. Col. Lindsay immediately ordered out the Dragoons and Artillery, and Major Yarborough soon followed with 2 companies of the 91st. They were hardly out of sight before it was perceived that they were engaged with the enemy. After a short time the gun was seen returning, one of the after horses having been shot dead. Soon afterwards Doctor Fraser[108] was seen galloping towards the post, to request the three-pounder and more ammunition, the Infantry being hard pressed by the Kafirs. The troops however nobly did their duty, and succeeded in beating them off, returning a little before sun-set. On this occasion the Dragoons had an opportunity of charging, and which they accomplished with considerable effect, about half of them returning with bloody swords. It is calculated that about 50 or 60[109] of the enemy were killed or wounded, whilst the only casualty on our side was one man slightly wounded in the arm.

Just at dark several parties of Kafirs were seen about the

Post. One party posted themselves in a kloof opposite the fort, and fired a few Fingoe huts. Five rockets were sent amongst them, and dispersed them. Another party came on the Post and fired on the picquet by the tower, into the horse barracks, and at the back of Capt. Maclean's, one ball actually striking over his head, as he was shutting one of the outside doors. A shot from the tower gun silenced them.[110] A few stragglers, however, kept skirmishing with the Fingoes till a late hour, sometimes taking cattle which were always recovered again. We slept in the fort ready to jump up at a moment's warning.

May 28th: The dreaded attack of the Kafirs has at length arrived, and, through the good Providence of God, passed off without a hair of our heads being touched. They came in four large bodies[111] and posted themselves on the heights for some time, thus giving us a good opportunity for making every preparation for their reception. The guns were all got in the best positions, and the outstanding picquets were called in, including the company of the 91st. who were over at the Station chapel. When they began to move, which they did in considerable order, it was evident that they intended to surround us, as they spread themselves out so as to meet on their arriving at the bottom. This however was in good part prevented by the first shot, which appeared not only to discomfort them, but to upset all their plans. The artillery kept up a continual roar for about an hour, by which time the immense masses were in full retreat. There was little opportunity for the play of musketry, as they fled as fast as they came within its reach. The few cavalry we had were at length ordered out, who soon cleared the ground of the stragglers without meeting any resistance. The ease with which the victory was won is truly astonishing, and can only be attributed to Divine assistance. In about two hours from the time that about seven thousand Kafirs began to move upon us, not one was to be seen, except perhaps a few stragglers in the distance. They belonged to every tribe, and doubtless constituted the strength of Kafirland. In the confusion of their first attack they managed to get off with most of the cattle, some of which, however, were retaken by the Fingoes who fought nobly on the occasion. The casualties on the Kafir side were 62 killed by the Fingoes, and perhaps as many more by the troops.[112] On our side 12 Fingoes were killed and 7 or 8 wounded, but not the hair of a white man was touched, though several balls whizzed over us, and 3 or 4 oxen close under the fort were killed.

One of our class leaders, George Sizaka was amongst the wounded, part of his skull being taken away by a bullet, but without injuring the brain. We were all in the fort, and I had thus a good opportunity of watching the whole engagement. The females and children were of course shut up in their usual nightly place of refuge. The Fingoe women and children sheltered themselves in the ditch[113] surrounding the fort. After all was over, and as the killed began to be known, it was truly heart-rending to hear the lamentations of their relatives. An awful accident occurred through the bursting of a shell close over the ditch as it left the cannon's mouth. A poor woman and her child were killed on the spot, being dreadfully cut, whilst another was wounded. In the case of three or four pregnant women, labour came on in consequence of their fright at the noise of the guns. Altogether it was an exciting time, and to God alone belongs the praise of our deliverance.

A few straggling parties tried to get off some more of the Fingoe cattle after dark, but without success.

May 29th : The cry was again raised this morning "the Kafirs are coming". On watching more narrowly, however, it was soon perceived, much to our comfort, that they were some of our own men, and turned out to be Capt. Donovan's troop of Cape Corps and Lucas's[114] troop of Burghers. It is calculated that the Fingoes lost about 4,000 head of cattle yesterday, including those of Jokwini's, Umyanda's,[115] the Beka station people's, some of Mr. Tainton's, as well as those of Umgai's.

May 30th: Nothing particular has occurred to-day. It is said by some of the Fingoes, that Dilima rode the white horse which was so conspicuous in last Thursday's engagement, and that they chased him a considerable distance, firing several shots at him at the same time though without any apparent effect. They say also that Ulisiba, one of Pato's wives' brother, was killed, and Katshaza[116]. It is reported also that Siwani[117] was killed in the Wednesday's engagement. Kota, one of Pato's counsellors, was killed in the Thursday's engagement.

May 31st: As I was preaching this morning the sound of cannon firing was heard in the direction of the Fish river, and was supposed to proceed from Col. Somerset's division, as we had heard that he was on his way hither. The service was immediately stopped, and the men ordered to fall in under arms. The Cape Corps and Lucas's burghers went out to reconnoitre, but returned without seeing anything.

A large party of Pato's Kafirs was observed to cross the wagon road this morning, and to go along the Bush higher up the Fish river.

June 1st: Some Fingoes came this morning from Trumpetter's with a few letters for the authorities here. They conveyed the intelligence that Col. Somerset had crossed Committees' drift,[118] and was on his way hither with a large number of wagons.[119] All the cavalry were ordered to proceed to Breakfast vley,[120] in order to render any assistance if necessary. A small party of Infantry was also despatched to Mt. Somerset. About midday Lieut. Bisset[121] arrived with some of the Cape corps, to request that oxen might be sent to replace some which were knocked up, and which was of course attended to. He stated that they had been attacked as they were ascending the hill, and that they were engaged with the Kafirs yesterday from 11 a.m. till sun-set, by which time they succeeding (sic) in getting all the wagons to the top of the bush. Two Fingoes and an English orphan lad of the name of (blank) were killed, and oxen, and horses. How many fell on the Kafir side is not known. Towards evening Col. Somerset arrived with 105[122] wagons, and 1,400 men.[123]

Two of the wounded Fingoes died last night.

June 2nd: I buried the poor English lad who was killed last Sunday, and whose remains were brought in by order of Col. Somerset.

All had been in bustle to-day with our large reinforcement.[124] Some spies are to go out this evening, to see where Pato can be best attacked, and to bring such information as they can pick up.

June 3rd: Very little intelligence as to the movements of the Kafirs. It is supposed that they have crossed the Keiskamma, and it is rumoured that Pato has done the same.

A part of the force here started for Trumpetter's to bring the wagons up, which arrived there several days ago.

June 4th: A large body of Kafirs was seen by the spies on the move last night, and is supposed to be proceeding to the Bush for the purpose of intercepting wagons. A party started from here last night to widen some portions of the road up the Fish river hill.[125]

June 5th: The wagons arrived from Trumpetter's this afternoon, without meeting the least opposition. No Kafirs in fact were seen. Two companies of the 90th arrived with them. Col. Somerset went out as far as the bush to meet them, and struck off towards the Gualana and the Beka, burning several Kafir kraals in his progress, and amongst them Pato's and Dilima's. They did not succeed in meeting with any Kafirs or cattle, though they were fired upon once from the bush near Pato's.

June 6th: The detachment of the 90th took possession of the chapel and part of the Mission House.[126] A Court Martial has been sitting to-day on Capt. C. Campbell for abandoning the wagons and retreating to Trumpetter's.[127] It sat also on Thursday.

June 7th: Some wagons started for the mouth of the Fish river,[128] but were recalled owing to the reception of fresh intelligence from Trumpetter's. Seven spans of oxen have been stolen from that post. Twenty-eight wagons are expected there to-night with supplies, which will have to be brought up by wagons and men from this place.

June 8th : A large force of Fingoes and others started last night for the Brack river, with orders to move on in the morning towards Stock's kraal, in order to co-operate with Col. Somerset, who was to meet them there. Col. Somerset had not been gone long before we heard a heavy cannonading and repeated vollies of musketry.[129] I rode out with Bro. Green to the edge of the bush leading up to Stock's kraal, which together with others the troops had set fire to. We saw them skirmishing with the Kafirs all through the bush, and saw them set fire to Eno's old place. After this they attacked a body of Umhala's people who were coming to the help of Stock. The Dragoons charged the whole mass, and the Cape Corps immediately followed on, so that there was a fearful carnage amongst the Kafirs. A more signal defeat was perhaps never experienced by them. Throughout the day from 300 to 500 must have been killed or severely wounded, whilst the only casualties on our side were two killed, namely a Fingoe and a Corporal of the Cape Corps, and ten or twelve wounded, including 3 officers. Two prisoners were taken, and are now on the Post. It is said that they can give us valuable information. One of them says that Sandili is in the Amatola mountains with the cattle, which he is to guard and defend. Umhala, Siyolo, and Pato are to keep this post poor, by preventing any supplies reaching it, and by and by to attack it a second time, and take the remainder of the cattle. Another story is that they were first to take possession of Trumpetter's.

Capt. Donovan had a narrow escape, being seized by some Kafirs, as he was entering the bush, and dragged down. Providentially one of Lucas's burghers was close at hand, who ran up and drew the Captain's sword, and ran it through two of them, by which time others had come up and completed his rescue.

Poor George Sizaka died last night, and I buried him this afternoon.

June 9th: About 20 wagons with supplies arrived safely from Trumpetter's, having met with no opposition.

Some parties went out to view the scene of battle. The dead lie about the Gwanga and onwards towards the Keiskamma in frightful numbers. Thirteen bodies were seen in the fountain where Mr. Tainton used to fetch water. Some were seen about the premises and amongst the ruins of the houses.

June 10th: It is said that Umhala returned home yesterday, and that most of the Kafirs have moved further off. The old prisoner says that the Kafirs whom the troops attacked on the flat, were the elite of Kafirland, a sort of invincible corps, and that they had been well furnished with guns and ammunition by the different tribes. Our station at Wesleyville was burnt about a fortnight since, but Mt. Coke was still standing on Sunday last.

June 11th: Some Boers went on a patrole this morning, and not seeing anything, imprudently off-saddled in a kloof, where they were soon fallen upon by a party of Kafirs. They lost 9 or 10 of their horses, and 2 of themselves were wounded, one badly.

Some Fingoes brought in a Kafir woman belonging to Stock's tribe. She says that Stock was persuaded to join the war party by his brother Sonto. Also that Stock's great Counsellor and many of the great men of the Amadhlambi, have been killed. Umgai has been talking to her, and will probably get some important information from her. Another troop of the 7th. Dragoons arrived to-day.

June 12th: Mr. Cumming, of the Commissariat, returned from the mouth of the Fish river, where a camp is now forming, with the intelligence that our Mission station at Newtondale is totally destroyed with the exception of the chapel, which is still standing.

We have received information that Zetu and Xamli, two chiefs of the Amadhlambi, as well as Hanisi, a noted rainmaker, and another great man belonging to the same tribe, were killed in the bush fight last Monday. It is said that in one kloof only, there were 80 dead bodies, and there have been counted no less than 184 in the neighbourhood of the Gwanga. Stock was at home on the day of the attack on the post, but all his people were here. Kobi, also, and his people were here. Last Monday Stock was at home, and only retired as the troops were approaching his place. On seeing his place set on fire, he cried out, "To-day I am ashamed of the Amabala"[130] and men were sent to find out Xala, who has been the chief instigator in exciting his people to join the war party, and it is supposed that he has been despatched.

Umgai thinks that the Amadhlambi will hardly fight again, after such a dreadful defeat. Some of his people have been found amongst the slain. At the fight on the flat they appear to have perished almost by families, it being said, that in one place a father and two sons, and in another a father and three sons, and so on, may be seen lying together.

The reports about the death of Mati,[131] and also that of Siwani, appear to be unfounded. It is said that very few of Stock's people were fighting last Monday, and that most of those in the bush were Umhala's men. This accounts for the exclamation of one of them heard during the fight, "Where are Stock's brave men to-day". The woman prisoner was in the bush during the fight, and near the place where Capt. Donovan was pulled down. She confesses that the Kafirs were so hard pressed, that they cried out for mercy. This they were heard to do by W. Shepstone and others.

June 13th: Col. Somerset started on another expedition last night, and will probably remain 2 or 3 days in the field.

Some more wagons arrived safely from Trumpetter's.

June 14th: An express arrived from Trumpetter's stating that the Governor was there, and intending to come on to-day. A strong escort was sent off early to meet him. He arrived about 4 o'clock, with his staff, and Col. Richardson. Soon after dark another train of about 30 wagons arrived safely with supplies.

About 10 wagons started for the mouth of the Fish river this morning.

Two Kafir women of Sonto's tribe came in towards evening, professedly at the instigation of Sandili, to inquire why the country was dead,[132] and why so many men were killed. They were probably merely spies.[133] Very little news could be got out of them. Umhala is said to have been in the same bush with Zetu, when the latter was killed.

June 15th: Sonto's two women, and also the one taken in Stock's country, were sent away to-day, with the assurance that if they ever came again, they would never see their country again. They were told that the Government only knew the name of Sandili, that he was only a ghost now.[134]

His Excellency rode out to Newtondale, to see the country in order as was supposed to the formation of Camps.

Intelligence came in from Col. Somerset. They have burnt nearly all the kraals between the Fish and Keiskamma rivers, captured about six or seven hundred cattle, and 100 goats, and killed a few Kafirs. They have had no engagement with the enemy, the Kafirs not venturing to face them.

Three women came in from Stock's, but pretended to know nothing.

June 16th: Stock's three women were sent off this morning, and also an old Kafir woman who has been staying here, the sister of Martha Ncinci.[135]

Mr. Brownlee, Mr. Green, and myself, went to see the Governor. Afterwards he saw Umgai, and expressed himself as satisfied with his conduct, and told him that he should not be forgotten.

Col. Somerset came in for a short time to-day, from the Gwalana, where he intends to form a camp. All has been in bustle with removing the wagons, &c., belonging to his division. Heard of the death of two more chiefs in the engagement of the 8th. inst., namely, John Ndhlambi,[136] and one of Gasela's sons.[137]

June 18th: Nothing of much moment has occurred either

to-day or yesterday. Col. Somerset continues at the Gwalana. The following list is considered a tolerably accurate estimate of the number of Kafirs killed, in their different encounters with the force at Fort Peddie. It is under-rated rather than over-rated.

April	23rd	4
,,	26th	1
,,	30th	3
May	6th	1
,,	8th	27
,,	21st	4
,,	27th	40
,,	28th	145
,,	31st	4
June	8th	364
,,	12th	6
On other occasions:		12
	Total	611

June 19th: The Governor and a large escort went out early this morning to bring up some wagons from Trumpetter's. A large signal fire was seen yesterday, and it was thought that the wagons might be attacked. No attack, however, was made.

June 20th: The Governor and his suite left to-day for the Fish river mouth, where the camp is to be formed for the present. A detachment is to remain at Newtondale, and Trumpetter's is to be 700 strong. The force left here amounts to about 300 under Col. Lindsay, including the Cape Volunteers.

By the post yesterday we learnt the melancholy tidings of the death of Rev. S. Palmer. This is truly an afflictive dispensation.

The Kafirs still plunder the Colony, and it is said that Tola is in the Fish river bush.

Notes and References

1. The incident which sparked off the war of the Axe occurred on 16 March 1846. D'Urban station was the obvious place to assemble owing to its proximity to Fort Peddie.
2. Son of Pato and brother of Mati, of the Gunukwebi clan.
3. i.e. Counsellors.
4. James Kidd, 1796– ?, an 1820 settler, catechist at Newtondale Mission. See E. Morse Jones, *Roll of the British Settlers in South Africa*, p. 134, C.T. 1969.
5. Rev. John Brownlee, of the London Missionary Society.
6. Stationed at Mt. Coke in 1846.
7. Joshua Webb, artizan stationed with Green at Mt. Coke.
8. See introduction, above, p. 35.
9. Martial Law was proclaimed in the same districts on 21 April.
10. Gaikas or western Xosa.
11. i.e. Eno or Nqeno. He died on 1 April at his kraal near Breakfast Vlei.
12. Son of Gaika and foremost of the chiefs of the Gaika tribes between the death of his father and Sandili's coming of age.
13. See introduction, above, p. 35. The proclamation was dated 21 March 1846.
14. Stock, son of Eno and brother of Sonto, was an Amambalu chief.
15. Major Yarborough, further unidentified.
16. This was correct. See introduction p. 36.
17. Lt.-Col. Lindsay, further unidentified.
18. Unidentified. Probably one of the Fingoe congregation.
19. No doubt Appleyard expected Lindsay to work through the Diplomatic Agent Capt. Maclean.
20. Capt. J. Maclean, 1810–74, of 27th Regiment.
21. This fight was known by the name of Burn's Hill. See introduction p. 36 and below, note 31.
22. Buck Adams was one of a party which buried 226 bodies of Xosa warriors on 9 April. See *The Narrative of Private Buck Adams*, VRS 22, p. 121. (Henceforth referred to as *Buck Adams' Narrative*).
23. Captain Bambrick was shot dead in his saddle on 15 April, *Buck Adams' Narrative*, p. 122–3. The Dragoons mentioned are the 7th Dragoon Guards.
24. The "room" was presumably within the Star Fort, in the immediate neighbourhood of the Commissariat store. See map, facing p. 5
25. See map, facing p. 5
26. Jokwini or Jokweni was one of the Fingoe chiefs, situated close to Newtondale. Map compiled by Mr. J. M. Donald of Peddie from S. G. sheets, aerial photographs and the Divisional map of Peddie of 1902.
27. Rev. J. F. Cumming, of the Glasgow African Missionary Society, which was separate from the Glasgow Missionary Society.
28. Unidentified. Probably one of Pato's men connected with the Wesleyans.
29. i.e. Umhala.
30. Tainton had been appointed by the District Meeting of January, 1846, to Port Natal to help W. J. Davis. It seems that the war interrupted his removal.
31. This occurred on 18 April, the day after the Burn's Hill defeat, on Somerset's retreat to Block Drift. See G. E. Cory *Rise of South Africa*, Vol. IV. p. 434.
32. A military observer said in 1820 of Xosa tactics: "As a body they are very weak; in detached parties and when acting in concert very redoubtable." Ives Stocker, Report upon Kaffraria, in G. M. Theal, *Records of the Cape Colony* Vol. XIII, p. 32 f.

The truth of this statement is nowhere better illustrated than at the Battle of Peddie. See below, p. 63 f.

[33] Fort Brown lies on the western bank of the Fish River, about 18 miles north-east, as the crow flies, from Graham's Town.

[34] Siyolo was a Dushani chief, brother of Siwane, who had given his allegiance to the Gaikas. See *Correspondence re Kaffirs, 1845-6*, 1847, XXXVIII [786] (Henceforth PP 786), p. 110: Capt. Maclean wrote to the Agent-General on 3 April 1846 to report that Seyolo "belongs to the Gaikas" and should be expelled from Ndhlambi land.

[35] i.e. his late father, Eno or Nqeno, who had enjoined his sons not to fight the English.

[36] Post Victoria was established in October 1843 in Tola's country to restrict his activities, by permission of the majority of Xosa chiefs. It was found ineffectual and was abandoned by Maitland at this time. See G. E. Cory, *Rise of South Africa*, Vol. IV pp. 370, 400, 437.

[37] This reference has not been confirmed.

[38] See above, p. 44.

[39] At the beginning of their stay in "Kaffraria" missionaries were granted a loan of £100 to buy cattle and they repaid this loan at the rate of £10 p.a. In the inventory of Appleyard's estate, 25 July 1874, mention is made of 12 oxen, valued at £90, and five cows and four calves valued at £35. He also had a small wagon with gear for 10 oxen. (Wills, Inventories and Appraisements, Cape Archives, MOOC No. 65.)

[40] Cory largely agrees with Appleyard's judgement on this incident. Two hours after the alarm had been given about two hundred men, consisting of two troops of the 7th Dragoon Guards, 60 of the 91st Regiment, a party of the C. M. R. and a few mounted burghers, taking with them two field pieces, left the Fort under the command of Lt.-Col. Richardson. Their action was ineffectual and Richardson soon retreated to Fort Peddie and left the Fingoes unassisted.

Lt.-Col. Lindsay, in command of Fort Peddie, reported that these men had marched on 29 April from Post Victoria and were not fit for service on 30 April. *Rise of South Africa*, Vol. IV p. 438.

[41] This press had been requested by the District Meeting in 1830 and arrived in Graham's Town in 1831. Owing to lack of the correct types, however, it was not in use until 1833 when William Shaw on his return to Britain sent out the correct types. P. J. Schutte *Sendingdrukperse in Suid Afrika, 1800-1875* D.Phil. (Bibl.) thesis, Potchefstroom, 1969. From 1834 the press was in constant use. Printers were difficult to come by. In 1840 the press was moved to the D'Urban station, and later to Newtondale.

A special note in the Minutes of the District Meeting of 13 January 1847 reads: "We think it calls for special and thankful acknowledgement to Divine providence that not only was the completion of the printing of the New Testament in Kaffir effected by the time anticipated in the minutes of last year, but the whole impression was safely transmitted from Newton Dale to Graham's Town and the printing press & type secured . . ." Appleyard could now proceed with "the complicated arrangements for the printing of the old Testament . . ."

[42] Nonibi was the great wife of Dushani and regent of the Imi-Dushani clan on his death.

[43] See above, p. 46.

[44] i.e. the Watchtower. See map, facing p. 5

[45] According to Munro the distance from Trumpetter's Drift to Fort Peddie "By road, or round by the Great Pass," was nearly twenty miles. There was a short cut which was negotiable to horsemen. W. Munro *Records of Service and Campaigning in Many Lands*, Vol. I p. 73.

⁴⁶ Unidentified.
⁴⁷ The citizens of Graham's Town considered that they were not sufficiently protected. They were defended, until Somerset arrived, by volunteers and Fingoes largely, and barricades had been thrown up. There was no attack on Graham's Town. Cory *Rise of South Africa*, Vol. IV p. 447.
⁴⁸ Maitland wrote to Lt.-Governor Hare that the war had become much more extensive than he had hoped and therefore he must take personal command of the troops. Maitland to Hare, 1 May 1846. Enclosure in Maitland's despatch to Secretary of State Gladstone, 15 May 1846. PP 786 p. 129.
⁴⁹ Presumably Fingoe kraals.
⁵⁰ His death is confirmed on p. 52, below.
⁵¹ Minor chief. See below, p. 52 note 64.
⁵² Son of the catechist at the Gwanga station and interpreter for his father. See list of Subordinate Paid Agents, Albany and Kaffraria Districts: annexure to the Minutes of the District Meeting of January 1843. The collection of firewood would have been a matter of great importance to Ford Peddie with its relatively high population density.
⁵³ This was the first of many attempts by Umkye to obtain the protection of the military. It seems that Siyolo had attacked Umkye. See below p. 55.
⁵⁴ The Imi-Dushani chiefs were Siyolo, Siwane and Fundisi, with Nonibi a chieftainess.
⁵⁵ Unidentified. See below, p. 56.
⁵⁶ "Brought away his kraal" probably means that they took his cattle and possessions to Fort Peddie.
⁵⁷ Probably W. G. B. Shepstone, although John Shepstone was also at Peddie. See Gordon, R. E. *Shepstone*, p. 73.
⁵⁸ This is probably the "Braake river" shown on James Wyld's map (*Graham's Town and the Out Posts*) as being a tributary of the Fish which lay between Fort Peddie and the drift at Trumpetter's.
⁵⁹ See note 46 above.
⁶⁰ See note 50 above.
⁶¹ A Fatherland cow is probably one of the Holstein-Friesian dairy breed.
⁶² The Xosa may mean "So great is the wisdom of Bodhla!" (translation by Mr. Jackson . . . of the Rhodes University Library staff). Presumably "Bodhla" is a proper noun which is indeterminate enough to refer to Umhala or his type.
⁶³ Appleyard later corrects this report: see below, pp. 53, 54 and 105. Cory carries only the early version, which is most damaging to Pato. See G. E. Cory, *Rise of South Africa*, Vol. IV p. 437, probably following J. Ayliff and J. Whiteside *History of the Abambo* (Fingos) p. 43.
⁶⁴ See also p. 55 below. Lama was evidently a minor chief living on the Brack or Braake river, between Fort Peddie and Trumpetter's Drift.
⁶⁵ The Gqutsho river referred to here is probably that which appears as "Goosha" on Mr. J. M. Donald's map of the Peddie District, compiled from S. G. sheets, aerial photographs and the divisional map of 1902. The Goosha passes close to Wesleyville, and between Wesleyville and Fort Peddie.
⁶⁶ i.e. Kobus.
⁶⁷ Rev. E. Scholtz of the Berlin Missionary Society's Dohne station, near the present Stutterheim, was attacked and killed near Fort Peddie in November 1845. He was travelling in one of Theophilus Shepstone's wagons and is thought to have died in his stead. G. E. Cory *Rise of South Africa* Vol. IV p. 410–11. Scholtz's grave lies about 100 yards from the old D'Urban mission station.
⁶⁸ There is a reference in R. F. Kennedy's *Africana Repository*, p. 108, to a portrait of a

"Kafir Jack". The portrait is attributed to I'Ons. It is possible, however, that "Kafir Jack" was a typical nickname.

69 The *Graham's Town Journal*, nicknamed "The Settlers' Bible", edited by Robert Godlonton. The remarks are unequivocal and include a condemnation of the incident as "most discreditable", and "one of the severest blows the Colony has yet received." The *Journal* called for a "rigid, searching enquiry," and presumes that Lt.-Col. Lindsay is guilty because of his known ineptitude for frontier fighting. Appleyard's description of the incident, on p. 46 above, differs from that of the *Journal* insofar as he states that shells were fired, whereas the report in the *Journal* categorically denies this. *Graham's Town Journal*, 9 May 1846.

70 Unidentified.

71 Dr. Macgregor was a "Staff-Assistant Surgeon" of the 91st Regiment. W. Munro, *Records of Service and Campaigning in Many Lands* Vol. I p. 45. He was evidently to attend the wounded at Trumpetter's Drift.

72 See above, p. 52, note 58.

73 See above, p. 52, note 64.

74 The details which follow apply to the engagement of 8 May. See above p. 52, and Cory *Rise of South Africa* Vol. IV p. 447.

75 i.e. Graham's Town.

76 The lime kiln has not been identified, but probably lay towards the Fish River, in a southerly direction.

77 See above p. 50, note 53. This incident has not been mentioned in Appleyard's text, but it goes far to explain Umkye's sudden arrival at Fort Peddie.

78 Unidentified.

79 The Tamara river is a short tributary of the Keiskama, entering that river from the east.

80 Nothing came of this.

81 If it was the place marked "Paradise, Lot 128", on Mr. J. M. Donald's map, then it was very close to the post. It lay to the south-west.

82 Both Amambalu chiefs and sons of Eno.

83 On chieftainship see also below, pp. 58, 61, 70, etc.

84 Presumably Major J. Campbell of 91st Regiment. See PP 786 p. 145, an enclosure from Campbell, dated Block Drift 13 May 1846.

85 See above p. 51.

86 See below p. 70 for the application of Sandili's idea to himself and all other chiefs, by Maitland.

87 See above, p. 40 note 7. Cattle were the most valuable of all possessions to the Xosa. Such a gesture as this was dramatic, though why they should be Webb's cattle in particular is not known. Perhaps they were in better condition than most.

88 Mt. Somerset is a hill just north of Fort Peddie.

89 This plan was not put into effect.

90 See above, p. 57.

91 Rili, Sirili or Kreli was paramount chief of the Gcaleka or eastern Xosa and this report would implicate the Gcaleka in the war. Such implication was never proved.

92 This rumour is unsubstantiated.

93 Maitland explained on 11 June to Secretary of State Earl Grey that he was still reducing the number of camps and outposts. He claimed that this policy would enable him the better to defend the exposed districts. His strategy was simple: "With the rest of the force I intend to advance from several points with strong divisions, communicating with each other; and by degrees work forwards, clearing the country by driving the Kafirs, step by step, to the east out of their strongholds." Maitland to Grey, 11 June 1846, PP 786 p. 144.

[94] Cory's account is summarised as follows: On Monday, 18 May, 43 wagons left Graham's Town "laden with necessaries, and including a large quantity of forage". The train reached Trumpetter's Drift on Tuesday. Lt. Dickson, in command at Trumpetter's Drift post, sent four civilians to Fort Peddie to ask Lt.-Col. Lindsay to send an escort to meet the train. On Thursday 21 May, Capt. Campbell of the 91st Regiment rode off to Trumpetter's Drift with 60 men.

Early on Thursday morning the wagons crossed the Fish river and soon they were joined by Campbell. Campbell took the bulk of the force to the rear and Dickson took a small advance party to the front of the wagons. After they had proceeded in this fashion for about two miles the Xosa attacked the front wagon, killing the oxen and immobilising the wagon. The second and third wagons were also lost when Dickson reported the arrival of 1,500 more Xosa. The whole escort collected in the rear after some bitter fighting and retreated to Trumpetter's Drift. The Xosa plundered and burnt the wagons. G. E. Cory *Rise of South Africa*, Vol. IV p. 448–9.

[95] Unidentified.

[96] See above, p. 40 note 7. Probably Joshua Webb, although there were by December 1854 three Webbs in the Peddie district. See Letters received from Resident Magistrate, L.G. 344, Cape Archives.

[97] i.e. D'Urban station.

[98] J. Harvey had been engaged in 1840 as printer and catechist at the Beka station, when the printing office was moved to D'Urban. Minutes of the District Meeting of 1 April 1840.

[99] Unidentified. Lt.-Col. Somerset had complained as early as 1836 of the nuisance of canteens near Military Posts. Somerset to Colonial Office, 11 July 1836. C.O. 455.

[100] The oat-hay store was presumably in the Cavalry barracks complex. See map, p. 00.

[101] See also above, p. 58.

[102] Established in 1843 by Sir George Napier as part of the chain of posts linking Fort Peddie to Graham's Town by semaphore. The scheme was a failure (see G. E. Cory *Rise of South Africa*, Vol. IV p. 371) and the Piet Apple watchtower was probably undefended at this time in accordance with Maitland's strategy. See above note 93.

[103] J. C. Smith.

[104] Cory gives a very similar version. John Crawford Smith was the son of one of the heads of the Settler parties of 1820. His father had been killed by the Xosa. He and other transport riders had contracted to ride supplies in to Fort Peddie.

Cumming, an officer of the commissariat at Fort Peddie, ordered Smith to take his wagon to a distant forest to cut wood. The mission was obviously dangerous and there was no mention of an escort being provided. With one accord the transport riders refused to go. Cumming reported the matter to Lt.-Col. Lindsay, the commanding officer, who offered to supply an escort. The transport riders then agreed to go but Lindsay decided to make an example of one of them for disobeying orders. He chose Smith, who received 25 lashes while tied to the wheel of a wagon.

One of the other waggoners, named Arrowsmith, begged for mercy for Smith but desisted when threatened with a similar punishment. There was a public outcry when this news reached Graham's Town and an action was commenced against Lindsay. It came before the Circuit Court in September 1847, where Judge Menzies decided that Lindsay had been justified under martial law in acting as he had done.

[105] Boards of relief for the destitute were set up generally by the Colonial Government. See enclosure of 15 May in Maitland to Gladstone, 15 May 1846. PP 786 p. 138. Probably Appleyard served on this particular board. See also Minutes of the District Meeting of 13 January 1847.

[106] See note 94 p. 59.

107 Unidentified.
108 Dr. Fraser is mentioned in W. Munro *Records of Service and Campaigning in Many Lands*, Vol. I p. 45 as being "Staff-Assistant-Surgeon". He is probably the same man as is mentioned in G. E. Cory, *Rise of South Africa*, Vol. IV p. 148.
109 Appleyard later estimates the number of Xosa killed in this skirmish to have been 40. See below p. 71.
110 According to Munro *Records of Service* . . . Vol. I p. 134, Lt. Patterson of the 91st Regiment and Lt. King R. A., were in charge of the artillery on 27 and 28 May.
111 It is interesting to compare Appleyard's version of the battle with the report of Lt. Col. Lindsay, the commanding officer. (Quoted in H. G. Robley and P. J. Aubin, *History of the 1st Battalion Princess Louise's Argyll & Southern Highlanders* (91st Regiment), p. 24):

> The first appearance of the Xosa: ". . . in three dense masses, with detached clumps of horses; other large bodies were also on the hills all round."
> The deployment of the troops immediately prior to the battle: ". . . The cavalry, with twenty artillery, were at the cavalry barracks and Star Fort, a sergeant's party at Mr. Webb's, and pickets in the officers, and engineers range."
> The action is described in the following words:
> "At twelve o'clock the whole of the enemy moved down to the post steadily preceded by clouds of skirmishers. When they came within range I directed Lieutenant King, R. A., to send a round shot at one of the masses, which killed three men. A shell was then thrown and a 12-pound rocket. The latter frightened the cattle, which rushed down towards the Kafirs, and were easily driven off by the Kafirs. The Fingoes pursued them, and succeeded in capturing a good number. The enemy so soon as they found our shots so well directed, scattered and got into the kloofs and hollows. One party of some hundreds got down the deep trench to Mr. Webb's house from which the detached party had been withdrawn, and began to plunder what little was left there by the owner; but a shell pitched into the yard, they quitted it, but got into the ditch and gardens about it, and fired at the barracks and fort without doing any injury, but several of their number were shot from the infantry barrack . . ."

112 Lindsay states that 92 dead bodies were reported and that the total loss on the Xosa side could be safely estimated at 200 killed and wounded. He differs from Appleyard in reporting that only two Fingoes were killed and three wounded. H. G. Robley and P. J. Aubin, *History of the 1st Battalion* . . . p. 24. Appleyard's own later estimate was 145 killed. See below, p. 71.
113 The ditch was that surrounding the Star Fort. Its position can still roughly be seen around the Church of St. Simon and St. Jude, Peddie. The Church building was originally the Commissariat store. Communication by Mr. J. M. Donald of Peddie.
114 Lucas was probably a settler of 1820, but cannot be identified.
115 Unidentified.
116 Unidentified.
117 Dushane chief, brother of Siyolo. Appleyard corrects this report below, p. 69.
118 Committees Drift was a ford across the Great Fish river, twelve miles north-east, as the crow flies, of Trumpetter's Drift.
119 104 wagons. The train spent the night of 30 May on the banks of the Fish river. The next day the advance guard was attacked while ascending Committees Hill. Buck Adams, who was in the escort, records that: "It was near sunset when we reached the summit of the Commitjees Mountain, having been 11 hours making a distance of less than nine miles." *Buck Adam's Narrative*, p. 140–41.
120 Breakfast vley or vlei lies to the north-east of Peddie, on the western side of the Keiskama.

[121] John Bisset, 1817–94, of the Cape Mounted Rifles. Author of *Sport and war: or recollections of fighting and hunting in South Africa* (1834–67), E. Morse Jones *Roll of the Settlers*, p. 92.

[122] Adams disagrees as to the number of wagons.

[123] Appleyard never refers to rations during the "siege". Adams claims that the soldiers at Fort Peddie had been "for the last ten days subsisting on 6 ounces of salt junk per day; no biscuit, meal, tea, coffee or vegetable of any kind." *Buck Adams' Narrative*, p. 144.

[124] For instance, Major J. C. H. Gibsone inspected all the cavalry. On the same day two divisions, each consisting of men of the 7th Dragoons and the C.M.R., had a smart encounter with Pato's men. The division to which Adams was attached returned on the evening of 3 June. *Buck Adams' Narrative* pp. 145–6.

[125] Presumably the "Great Pass" referred to by Munro (see above p. 48 note 45) between Fort Peddie and Trumpetter's Drift.

[126] i.e. D'Urban station.

[127] See above, pp. 59 and 62.

[128] This is the first indication in Appleyard's text of the attempt by the military to avoid the Fish River Drifts by landing supplies on the coast to the east of the Fish River mouth and transporting them by wagon to Fort Peddie from the coast. Maitland to Gladstone, 18 September 1846. PP 786 p. 154.

[129] This action led to the famous "battle of the Gwanga", probably the most successful cavalry action on the Eastern frontier. Cory's version is summarised as follows:

Somerset's attack was originally meant as a feint to attract the attention of the Xosa while a convoy of empty wagons set out for Graham's Town.

On Sunday night, 7 June, Hottentots and Fingoes were sent out on patrol in the area. At 6.00 am. on Monday Lt.-Col. Somerset took a troop of 7th Dragoon Guards, 100 C.M.R., about 200 of the burghers from George and some native levies, on patrol. His artillery consisted of two six-pounders, two twelve-pound howitzers and a rocket tube.

The first engagement with the enemy lasted about five hours. The Xosa were dispersed and Somerset was then joined by Hottentot and Fingoe levies and proceeded to burn Stock's kraals. The first engagement had been with Umhala's men.

Somerset then moved towards the Gwanga, a small tributary of the Keiskama and there chanced upon not Umhala's men as Appleyard says, but Siyolo's, in open country. Major Gibsone and Captain Sir Harry Darell led the Dragoons into the Xosa mass and when the action ceased there were 270 Xosa corpses on the field. The Colonial losses were as Appleyard states.

Cory says three prisoners were taken. G. E. Cory *Rise of South Africa* Vol. IV p. 458–9. Sir Harry Darell's sketch of the action, reproduced in Cory, ibid., opposite p. 459.

[130] or Amambalu, his clan.

[131] See below, p. 81.

[132] "the country is dead" is an expression which means that there is a state of war prevailing.

[133] There were to be many more like them.

[134] i.e. that he was not recognised as a chief.

[135] Unidentified.

[136] Probably a Ndhlambi chief of minor rank.

[137] Ndhlambi chief ("Gazella" in Cory, *Rise of South Africa* Vol. IV p. 354.)

Introduction to Chapter IV

During the remaining months of 1846 Maitland was faced with the problem of ending hostilities and making another settlement on the Eastern Frontier. His military task was facilitated by the unwillingness of most of the Xosa to fight at a time when they felt they should be planting their crops. But Maitland went further: he tried to alter the structure of Xosa society in his effort to create a durable settlement.

An attack on chieftainship lay at the root of Maitland's civil policy. He attempted to wean from their hereditary chiefs the men of the various tribes by allowing individuals to surrender. As individuals they would then be registered and given land where the colonial authorities thought they should have it. By September Maitland believed that he had "shattered the hostile tribes, and broken to pieces their organization as communities".[1]

Some kind of authority there must be among the thousands of individuals, and Maitland proposed to create a hierarchy which looked very much like the existing one. In the end he found that there was no alternative to the old hereditary chieftainship. In any case, the new Secretary of State in charge of the colonies, Earl Grey, had decided that the chieftainship should be supported and the chiefs and their men manipulated into a position where they could serve the Colony.

Grey sent Sir Henry Pottinger to replace Maitland. Pottinger had had experience in India which might aid him in implementing Grey's new policy. But he was faced with a renewed outbreak of hostilities early in 1847 and by the end of the year he had left the Cape for Madras.

The Xosa chieftainship, in the midst of this vacillation, escaped unscathed. The tribesmen and their chiefs knew how to look after their own. They were relentless negotiators and, as Appleyard saw, even a beaten and friendless chief was a match for Maitland.

Appleyard was no longer at the centre of affairs. Military Headquarters had moved eastwards. However, the central issues are still reflected in the Journal and it seems that Appleyard was kept in touch with affairs by

Shaw and Maclean, both of whom had direct access to the Governor. Probably his most valuable comments are those on the cattle-stealing, spying and other subterfuges employed by the Xosa.

Notes and References

[1]Maitland to Gladstone, 18 September 1846. PP 786 p. 157.

Chapter IV

The War of the Axe (ii)

June 21st : Had our services as usual, except that an additional one was held at the Station for the Cape Volunteers, who have taken up their quarters there.

Kobi's sister and two other women were found lurking about as spies, and brought in by the Fingoes. They pretended to have a message from Pato, to ask what the war was about, and why it was continued so long. The truth is, probably, that they came to find out where Somerset was, and what he was intending to do.

We have heard again that Mati is killed, and that Pafa[1] was shot through the thigh. Also that both Xosa and his son have been killed, the former at Theopolis.[2]

June 22nd : Firing was heard this morning in the direction of Stock's country, and also from the sea-coast. Went to see the three women prisoners with Green and Tainton, but we could make nothing of them.

A party of Provisionals[3] and Fingoes arrived this evening with a few cattle which they had taken in Stock's country. They left Trumpetter's early this morning and came up through the bush. They saw about 500 Kafirs who kept at a great distance, though they had some sort of fighting with them. Six Kafirs were killed, and some wounded, but there was no casualty on our side.

June 23rd : The two men prisoners, and the three women prisoners, were sent off to Graham's Town to-day.

A shocking accident occurred to one of the Cape Volunteers, a young man of the name of Wright,[4] being accidentally shot by one of his companions. He died in about 3 hours.

June 24th : A very old woman came in this evening pretending to be on a journey from Stock's country to Pato. She was of course taken prisoner as a spy, this being doubtless a new mode of trying to gather information.

Firing was heard in the direction of the Fish river.

June 28th: Preached this morning to the troops, and in the afternoon to the Cape Volunteers.

Nothing of any moment has occurred the last few days. Firing has been heard in the direction of Beaufort, and it is supposed that Col. Hare has entered Kafirland with his division. Col. Somerset is about to remove his camp 5 miles inland, leaving Major Yarborough with about 200 men of the 90th and 91st Regts. at the mouth of the Fish river, where a post is to be formed, called after the Admiral of this Station, Fort Dacres.[5]

June 29th: The Governor came in this afternoon from the camp, leaving Col. Somerset with the cavalry at the Gwalana. The Marines and Sailors have been ordered back to their ships, owing it is understood to some disturbance at the Mauritius.

June 30th: Col. Somerset and his party passed by to-day on their way to the Gwanga, where they are to encamp for the night, with the intention of proceeding to Stock's country in the morning, and where they are to cooperate with different bodies of infantry, who are to proceed thither by different routes, so as to sweep the country between them.

From a letter from home I learnt the death of Cousin Frank[6] in India, and am truly thankful to find, that there is every reason to believe he died in the Lord.

July 1st: Stock's country received a thorough sweeping to-day. Few Kafirs, however, were seen, most having it is supposed vacated the country and proceeded higher up the river. Some women were caught in the bush, who said that Stock was anxious to clear himself, but did not know how to communicate with the Government. It is understood that His Excellency told them that he did not receive what they stated as a message from Stock, but that if Stock wished to clear himself he might come to Fort Peddie to-morrow with his wives and 1 man, and then he would hear what he had to say. He gave them also to understand they would not be permitted to occupy their country again. A few cattle and goats were captured in the bush, and all the remaining huts burned. One or two Kafirs were shot.

July 2nd: Col. Somerset's party passed through this morning on their return to the camp at the Fish river. His Excellency has also returned with them. If they had a sufficient quantity of supplies, the forces would now be able to march into Kafirland. As it is they are sadly crippled for the want of them, and transport is exceedingly difficult to be obtained. Their next move will probably be into Pato's country.

July 3rd: Stock's sister with two other women came in this evening, to say that Stock was sitting still, and to try, I suppose, to get a favourable word from the Government. His guilt, however, is too well established for the Government to show any more favour to him than to another.

July 6th: Yesterday 450 Fingoes of this settlement, headed by Mr. W. Shepstone, started for the Beka mouth, where they are to meet the division under Col. Somerset, and thence proceed with them to Kafirland. This evening we returned to our former quarters at the Mission House, D'Urban, where we shall be able to breathe a little, after being penned up so long in one room.

    I hope I shall now be able to pursue my studies with something like regularity.[7] I intend to devote a little time to Greek and Hebrew, which I have sadly neglected since my arrival in Africa.

July 7th: Through two Kafir women who have been staying here, and who took it into their heads to accompany Stock's sister home for some purpose or other, we have learnt that Stock and all his people are still in the bush, and that they defy the English to drive the Amambalo away. They are in a deep ravine with all their cattle and horses, through which the Irura[8] river flows, and not far from Stock's place, and here they were quietly ensconced when all our troops were there on the 1st instant, and yet not discovered. It is a pity that the Governor does not leave Col. Somerset to act alone. He is every way qualified for the work, and the presence of his Excellency will only tend to cramp him, and perhaps make him dogged.

July 9th : Three of Stock's women came in again this evening with a message from Stock to the Government, stating that he was ashamed of himself, of his conduct, and of his people, that he had made his friends ashamed, &c., and asking for mercy, or rather apologising for not having come out to meet the Governor when the troops were in his country. Capt. Maclean says in answer that if he chooses to come and give himself up as a prisoner of war, and go to Graham's Town, he shall be taken care of, but that for his people no distinction can be made between them and others, being equally guilty.

July 14th : Umgai and all his party left for Graham's Town this morning, 31 in all. He had gone on his own request on the ground of fear for his life, believing that one object of Stock's messengers is to find out his sleeping place, in order to plan his assassination now that the post is left so weak.

Nothing has been heard from the camp the last few days. Col. Somerset's division is now about 4 000 strong.[9] They are probably at the Keiskamma.

July 16th : Firing of musketry was heard in the direction of Stock's country. On riding out several fires were also seen, but no troops. Supposed to be Capt. Hogg's[10] party falling upon Stock's people.

July 18th : Several wagons arrived from the Fish river with ammunition and supplies. Intelligence has also reached us of the arrival of Col. Somerset's division at the mouth of the Buffalo, after a tedious march along the coast, on the 16th instant. No Kafirs were fallen in with, but they were seen driving off their cattle, and are supposed to have crossed the Buffalo. A spirit of complaint appears to generally prevail, at the slowness and uncertainty of the military proceedings. Three months have now passed over since war was

War Dance in a Fingoe Settlement

proclaimed, and yet nothing has been accomplished of any moment in the prosecution of the war.[11]

July 20th: Received further intelligence of the movements of the troops from a letter from Mr. Lucas. He had visited the Jamjam[12] and Wesleyville. At the former place he found an old woman, who stated that Pato had gone with all his people and cattle across the Kei. Wesleyville he found in ruins, not a vestige of any thing remaining but part of the walls. Old Joseph, the Interpreter, and Spochter[13] left about a month since for the Kei, being afraid to come towards the Colony, lest the Kafirs should kill them. Wesleyville was destroyed by a party on their way to Pato's place. Joseph remonstrated with them, and thereby endangered his life. The troops were to start again in a day or two for Umhala's country, and thence, it is supposed, to proceed to the Amatola mountains. It is said that the Kafirs have assembled in immense numbers at Sirili's[14] place, where they intend to make a stand against the troops.

July 22nd: Heard the Kafir account of last Thursday's firing through Martha Ncinci's sister, who was sent out by Capt. Maclean. It was a party, as supposed, from Committees',[15] but they did not succeed in driving Stock or his people away. Three Kafirs were killed and 1 woman wounded. Several women were driven out of a kloof, and stripped of their karosses.

A herd of Fingoe cattle were stolen by a few Kafirs this afternoon. They were feeding at some distance from the Post, and were herded by only two or three boys. A man, however, happened to be with them at the time, and upon his running away, the Kafirs cried out to him not to run away, as they were not going to kill him, because they knew he was the only man remaining at Peddie.

July 23rd: Some more women of Stock's came in last night, with a messenger to beg earnestly for mercy. They returned again this morning with a message similar to what he received before. They stated that he has altogether separated from the war party, and that he is now sitting upon his father's grave,[16] with only 8 or 9 followers & their families. Should Stock come in and lay down his arms as a prisoner of war, together with his followers, it is proposed to let them have a kraal & bring in their cattle & goats, so that they may be able to maintain themselves.

July 24th : Col. Johnson[17] with a part of the 27th Regt. and a good number of Dutch & Hottentot Burghers arrived to-day. They are going on in the morning to the Gwanga, & thence to the Tamara, where, it is understood, they are to meet Col. Somerset, who has now a separate division, the Governor taking one himself.

Stock has not arrived to-day, as some expected.

July 28th : This morning an express arrived, and afterwards Mr. Shepstone, bringing intelligence from the Green river[18] camp, where the Governor & Col. Somerset, as well as Col. Johnson, had arrived with their respective divisions. Col. Hare was to attack Makomo's kraal yesterday morning, and proceed to the Debi[19] flats, where the Governor intends to concentrate his forces, in order to carry out his plan of operations.

It appears that Col. Somerset left the Buffalo, with about 1 500 men, including our Peddie Fingoes, and reached the Kei on Sunday night. On Monday morning he attacked some Kafirs who were prepared to dispute his crossing the river, and who dared them to come on. No sooner however, did our troops, principally Fingoes, make a dash at them, than they fled in confusion. About 5 600 head of cattle were captured, several Kafirs killed & wounded, and 3 were taken prisoners. Col. Somerset had three shots fired from the cannon, and informed the prisoners that one was intended for Sirili, and was a declaration of war against him for having harboured Pato, the great enemy of the Colony, another was for Umhala, and another for Pato. By those three shots he also took possession of the country from the Kei to the Fish river, in the name of the British Government. He was now going back to attack the Gaikas, but when they were subdued, he should return and sweep their country.[20] With this he let the prisoners loose, who kissed his feet, and quickly departed, and would no doubt soon spread the information they had received. From these prisoners they learnt that Pato was at the Gqunubi,[21] in some of the ravines near the coast, and that Umhala was at another river not far off. It is said by the Kafirs that Umhala lost 500 men at the Gwanga affair, and that now he is left without assistance from the other tribes, because he held himself aloof at first and acted independently. The Kafirs are making fortifications in the fastnesses of the Amatola. King William's Town[22] is destroyed, and also Mt. Coke, except that the walls of the new house are still in being. Mr. Brownlee's[23] books were lying about in a tattered condition. It is feared that Jan Tshatshu[24] has given in to the war party. His house was the only one standing when the troops arrived, and they completed the scene of desolation by burning it. He has written again to Col. Hare, and at the close of his epistle he adds, this must be put in the paper, the word must being underlined. In his house the "Wrongs of the Kafirs"[25] was found, inscribed Miss Mary Tshatshu from her sincere friend . . . . . This volume is in the possession of Capt. Maitland,[26] and who was desired by His Excellency to take special care of it. Who Miss Mary Tshatshu's friend is, I did not hear, but think it very likely to be Dr. Philip.

About 300 Fingoes arrived with between two & three thousand cows & calves, which are to be distributed in the Settlement. Since the capture of the cattle, there has been fighting every night, and several Kafirs have been killed. At the Kei, and coming down, about 50 or 60 Kafirs are supposed to have been killed. The only casualties on our side are 1 Boer wounded, and I believe a Fingoe killed, but not of this settlement. Sixteen wagons arrived with supplies on their way to the Camp. Other wagons are on their way to the Fish river from the camp. This convoy was attacked by the Kafirs, but without success. Siyolo still clings to his country. He says, he wants more sugar and coffee, and shall not leave his nest. Unless he be routed out, therefore, every convoy will most likely be attacked, and a large escort will be required through the Keiskamma.

July 29th: Last night 3 mounted Kafirs succeeded in getting a span of oxen from the Post, but they were fortunately intercepted by the Fingoes before they got beyond the Kraals.

It appears that Col. Johnson is encamped between the Keiskamma and the Tamara, and not at the Green river as I had understood. It is said also that Siyolo is with Sandili, and that there are only stragglers of different tribes who continue in that part of the country.

It is said that Faku[27] is at the Bashee, and that Mr. T. Shepstone is with him.

Heard that Siwani, son of Umhala; an old man who was brother to Eno; and Benjesi, who was formerly a member at Mt. Coke, were amongst the slain on the 8th of June.

July 31st: This evening firing was heard in the direction of the Gwanga, and which proved to be an attack made upon a party of Dragoons and Cape Corps, who were bringing in some horses and a wagon from the Camp.

August 1st: It appears that the Kafirs were firing upon the party who came in last night, almost all the road from the Keiskamma to Mt. Somerset. All the mischief they effected, however, was the wounding one horse. Col. Johnson has left the Keiskamma, and joined Col. Somerset. It was reported that firing was heard in the direction where Col. Hare was supposed to be, and that fires had been seen on the tops of the Amatola. The Governor & Col. Somerset were to move yesterday into the Mountains, and that an attack would be made to-day.

August 3rd: Sir H. Darrell's[28] troop of Dragoons and some Fingoes left last night with 10 wagons for the Camp, but returned again this afternoon, the escort being considered insufficient for the Keiskamma drift, where it was reported several Kafir fires had been seen.

August 4th: An express was sent off in the night to the Governor's camp with the above information. Several wagons arrived from the Fish river, and are to go forward as soon as intelligence arrives from the Camp.

August 8th: An Express arrived last night from the Camp near Fort Beresford,[29] ordering the wagons to move on. No Kafirs were seen either going or coming, and it is understood that the Governor has expressed his surprise that they were not forwarded before, considering the large force which he had left here. Col. Hare and Sir. A. Stockenstrom had moved towards the Amatola mountains, and had encountered some of the Kafirs, but had taken no cattle. It is reported that the enemy are panic struck at the advance of the troops, and have fled into Sirili's country beyond the Kei, and whither it is supposed our troops will have to follow them.

August 11th: Col. Somerset arrived at the Gwanga yesterday, where he will put up for winter quarters, to recruit his horses. Col. Richardson is also with him. The Amatolas have been scoured, but nothing decisive accomplished. The Governor & Stockenstrom have moved on with about 4 000 Infantry, and intend to cross the Kei. Col. Hare is resting at Fort Cox,[30] and Col. Johnson at Fort Beresford. It is thought that there will not be another general move till October. In the mean time supplies will be got together. The Kafirs have burnt an immense tract of country.[31] It is said that the best part of their cattle have been sent to the sources of the Tsomo.[32]

August 22nd: Nothing of particular moment has occurred the last few days, except messages from Stock which have terminated in his surrender to Col. Somerset to-day.[33] We rode out to the camp at the Gwanga this morning, and arrived just in time to see Stock and 42 followers coming in with the white flag. After a little conversation Stock gave up his gun to Col. Somerset who soon afterwards returned it to him. The other men then gave up their arms, consisting of 33 guns and 36 assegais, all of which have been retained. He was then given till to-morrow evening to bring in his family, and such other of his people as were willing to comply with the same terms, after which his country would be scoured, and of course all found therein must take the consequences. Capt. Maclean started with an escort for the Governor's camp, to inform him of what had taken place, and to get his decision as to what was to be done with Stock in this new position of affairs, and which may be considered as the first step towards peace. Stock is to restore all colonial cattle and horses taken by his people in one month.

It appears that the Governor has remained at Fort Beresford, and that Col. Johnson and Stockenstrom have gone across the Kei, with orders to return by the 10th. of the next month.

August 24th : Col. Somerset started this morning to scour the country between this and Fort Wiltshire, and by this means to open the road to Fort Beaufort, in order to send supplies thither from the Fish river. A post is also to be established in the neighbourhood of Fort Willshire.

August 25th : Capt. Maclean returned yesterday from the Governor's camp with the Governor's remarks and orders in reference to Stock. We rode out to the Gwanga to hear them delivered to Stock, who had with him about 73 men. The substance of what His Excellency decided upon is contained in the following particulars:-

1. That Stock was not only to return such colonial cattle and horses as had been taken by his people, but that he would be required in due time to pay his share with the other chiefs of the expense consequent upon the destruction of property in the Colony and Kafirland.

2. That no Kafir would ever be permitted to live between the Fish and Keiskamma rivers, except Kama.

3. That the Kafirs would not be permitted to live between the Keiskamma and Kei rivers, but that country would be occupied by the troops till free from them.[34]

4. That Stock might come with two followers, and their families, to Peddie, under the surveillance of the Agent, the

same privilege being extended to Eno's widows & old counsellors, but that all his other people both men and women, must immediately go beyond the Kei, where they should not be molested by the troops. If Stock refused to go to Peddie, he also must go with his people beyond the Kei.

After some conversation Capt. Maclean gave Stock till 12 o'clock to-morrow, to come to a decision as to what course he intended to adopt. He appeared to feel very much on the position in which he found himself placed, it being evidently a more stringent one than he expected, though not more so than he deserves. He has in fact been playing a most treacherous part. His illness has been all feigned. He joined the war party of his own accord by his own confession.[35] Whilst he was here on the 21st of May, his people were attacking the wagons which were burnt and plundered on that day.[36] They were his people also who attacked Col. Somerset's wagons as they were coming from Committees'.[37]

August 26th: Stock has determined to come to Peddie with Eno's old counsellors & widows, and two or three followers. He pleaded hard that all the men who had come in with him the first day, should be permitted to live with him. But Capt. Maclean was firm, and refused to allow them, abiding by the Governor's orders. To-morrow the case of the women and children is to be decided.

August 27th: Stock has come in to-day with about 20 men, and about 80 women and 70 children. The rest are to proceed over the Kei, and to commence their journey to-morrow morning. Stock has also delivered up his gun which Col. Somerset returned to him, for the Governor, as an additional proof of his submission to the Government.

August 31st: Firing heard in the direction of the Gwalana. Conference with Stock. He is permitted to live between the Kwelera[38] and Kei riviers as a temporary arrangement. He leaves two men as hostages for the fulfilment of the conditions of peace, and also his mother with a girl to wait on her. About a hundred head of cattle were carried off this afternoon from the Settlement. Men followed on the spoer as far as the Keiskamma, but did not recover them. We were all alarmed in the evening by the hearing of fire-arms & the screaming of women, but it turned out to be the men returning from the pursuit of the cattle, some of whom foolishly fired off their guns on coming near the Station.

Heard that Mapassa's kraal had been surrounded, his cattle taken, 9 men killed, and he himself taken prisoner.[39] Also that Capt. Hogg's party had fallen upon some of his people, and captured 4 or 5 thousand cattle, besides killing nearly 100 of them.

Col. Somerset returned from his patrole but without doing much. The Kafirs fled as soon as seen. About 9 were killed & about 100 trek oxen were captured.

A party of about 60 Boers passed through on their way to the Fish river, where they are to remain & patrole the country, as the Kafirs are beginning to be very daring in that part.

September 1st: Stock and his party started this morning for their temporary residence at the Kwelera. Col. Somerset left the Gwanga with an escort for the Governor's camp. An express came in to-day from His Excellency, but the intelligence is vague.[40] It is said that Col. Johnson & Sir A. Stockenstrom have captured about 6 000 head of cattle, supposed to belong to the Gaikas, and that the latter has patched up a sort of peace with Sirili.[41] A council of war, it is rumoured, is to take place on Friday, and it is said that Sandili and other chiefs will have a hearing on that day. May the Lord give wisdom at this crisis of affairs.

A Mr. Smith[42] came in from Newtondale for 1 500 rounds of ammunition. The firing heard yesterday proceeded from a patrole from that place. They fell in with some Kafirs and killed 2 of them. Newtondale is to receive an additional strength of 100 burghers.

September 2nd: The report about Mapassa being taken prisoner turns out to be incorrect. It was another person, and who is believed to be the man who murdered young Aldum.[43]

Another herd of cattle has been carried off to-day by the Kafirs.

One of the men whom Stock has left behind has given information of his having hidden some meal. He has also let out that Stock was at the fight on the 27th of May,[44] and that one of the Dragoons made a slash at him with his sword, which he only just evaded, and then made off.

September 12th : Nothing of much moment has occurred the last few days. Some sort of council appears to have been held at the Governor's camp, during which Stockenstrom's patched-up peace with Sirili was annulled.[45] No chiefs were there except Stock, who has obtained permission to live near the Tamara for the present. A large patrole was out on Tuesday towards Fort Wiltshire, but returned unsuccessful, having captured only two or three horses and oxen and a few goats.

Yesterday both the Governor's and Col. Somerset's divisions passed through Peddie. They are all going to encamp at Newtondale for a short time to recruit their oxen and plan future operations.

The Kafirs are again very troublesome in the colony. Some herds have lately been killed, and cattle carried off, from near Graham's Town. Towards Beaufort things are in a deplorable state.

September 16th : Yesterday some more cattle and goats were carried off by the Kafirs, but were retaken by the Fingoes supported by a few Dragoons, and one Kafir killed. Mr. Castray accompanied the Dragoons, and on his return examined the Beka premises, when he found that everything had been burnt with the exception of a table & part of a door, nothing but the bare walls of the house & other buildings being left. Boozak, one of our native members of Mount Coke, arrived with a message from Umhala, which was immediately forwarded to the Governor, who has removed to the neighbourhood of Waterloo Bay.[46] Umhala is living at the

Nxarune[47] and appears to be tired of war and its consequences. His people, however, refuse to submit to Government upon the terms proposed.

Col. Somerset was to start to-day on a patrole up the Keiskamma. Some Fingoes are to join him at the Nyulusi[48] to-morrow from here.

The Governor has sent for Mr. Shaw to advise him on the present state of affairs.[49]

September 19th: Boozak returned yesterday to Umhala with the Governor's message, and also one from Mr. Shaw, who came from the Governor's camp to talk with him. His Excellency continues firm, and will only grant peace on the condition of laying down his arms. If he chooses to do this, he can come to Fort Peddie with as many of his people as are willing to follow his example, when he will be given a small tract of country for a temporary residence as in the case of Stock.

The general plan for the future settlement of the country is something like the following. The country between the Fish & Buffalo rivers to be filled up with native settlements of Fingoes, Hottentots, Mozambiquers,[50] and Kama's Kafirs, with perhaps three or four European towns in connexion with Military posts. The country between the Buffalo and the Nxarune to be neutral territory, that is, unoccupied. The country between the Nxarune and the Kei, to be occupied, on sufferance, by such Kafir chiefs and their people as are willing to be placed under British controul. All the other Kafirs must retire beyond the Kei, which will be the future boundary of our British territory in this part of South Africa.[51]

September 22nd: A beautiful rain yesterday and Sunday. Col. Johnstone encamped with his men on the station last evening, but moved on again this morning. He is on his way to take the command of the first division, Col. Hare having been obliged to resign on account of ill health.[52] An express passed through from Col. Somerset to the Governor. He is somewhere about Wesleyville. He has captured 15 horses and 150 cattle, killed 3 or 4 Kafirs and taken 4 prisoners, from whom he thinks he has learnt the whereabouts of Pato.

Kama and Hermanus[53] with about thirty followers arrived on the post. They are proceeding to the Governor's camp, being sent for in connexion with some of the future arrangements.

September 29th : Col. Somerset has met with further success, having captured about 1 100 head of cattle and 30 horses.

Kama has returned from the Governor's camp, on his way home. He has the promise of the country between Fort Willshire and Block Drift.

Mr. Shaw was to return home yesterday from the Governor's camp. He has received authority to settle some natives for the present season at Newtondale, and he has desired me to prepare to take charge of them.[54]

Mr. Calderwood[55] has been commissioned to offer the same terms of peace to Maqomo as were made to Stock.

October 3rd : Returned from Waterloo Bay whither we proceeded on the 30th ult. to procure supplies, of which we were all getting very short.[56] Col. Somerset has returned from his patrole with about 5 000 head of cattle and nearly 100 horses. He went as far as the mouth of the Gqunubi, and found that many of the Kafirs had ploughed. He met with very little resistance. He heard that Pato was living at the Kwelera.[57]

October 8th : By the post from Graham's Town we learn that a meeting had taken place between Col. Johnson and the Gaika chiefs, and that our terms of peace had not been accepted by the latter.[58] Kama's opinion on the matter is probably correct, namely, that they only want peace in order to plough and reap, & then they would be for war again. English news had also arrived up to August 9th. The Colonial cause had been taken up warmly at home. Two regiments had been ordered out in July, and 5 ships were chartered to sail in August with some others, so that before long we may expect to have a sufficient force to bring hostilities to a speedy conclusion.

October 16th: Every thing appears to be now in statu quo. It seems probable that the Buffalo mouth will be soon taken up as a landing place for supplies, and that a camp will be formed there.

October 19th: Boozak came on Saturday evening, but brought no message from Umhala, whom he had not seen since Col. Somersets patrole was in his vicinity. Boozak has returned with his family to Mt. Coke. In that neighbourhood the Kafirs are generally returned to their places to plough, imagining that as the troops have retired it is now peace.

Some of Jan Tshatshu's people also came on Saturday night, bringing a letter or two from him to Mr. Brownlee, but no message to Government. Under such circumstances Capt. Maclean ordered them off yesterday morning.

October 20th: An express from Fort Beaufort. Maqomo was to have given up his guns yesterday & it was supposed that Sandili would follow his example.[59]

Stock brought in 48 cattle and 6 horses as the plunder taken by his tribe from the colonists. Most of the cattle are oxen, and have every appearance of being those which the commandoes were obliged to leave behind, through poverty of condition. It remains to be seen whether our present Governor will submit to be duped by such impudent shuffling as this.

October 22nd: The Governor's answer to Stock arrived, and expresses dissatisfaction with the cattle, and the Governor only receives them as a portion, not as a whole. He has given Stock permission to live near Mount Coke, but he is not to trespass on the country within 5 miles of the Mouth of the Buffalo, this being intended as a reserve for a Military Post. Stock objects to this on the ground of insecurity, and asks permission to come this side of the Keiskamma.

October 24th: An answer arrived from the Governor, giving Stock permission to live between the Beka and the Tua[60] rivers, but as a report had been brought in that the Newtondale cattle had been carried off by two of Stock's men, as they were returning from the Governor's camp, Capt. Maclean held the permission back till he heard again from His Excellency.

October 26th: This morning Stock and his men were assembled, and a trial took place in reference to the stolen cattle. A little Hottentot boy who was herding them at the time, swore to two of the men present as those who took the cattle. These have been imprisoned and the spoer given over to 4 of Stock's men. The others were ordered off at once, whilst Stock and 4 followers remained till an answer arrived from the Governor. This took place soon after the trial. His Excellency informs Stock that he must remain at the Shushu[61] near the Tamara, and expects that he will at once get the cattle restored with payment. Unless this is done, he is to expect no favour from the Government.

An express passed through for Beaufort. It is rumoured that Col. Johnstone has committed a serious blunder.[62]

October 30th: The Governor arrived yesterday, and left this morning for Block Drift, where it is said he will have a meeting with Maqomo and other Gaika chiefs. The 45th regiment also arrived yesterday and left for the same part to-day.

Nonibi sent in 4 women to ask for peace. Two boys who have left Pato's people came here a day or two since. They say that Pato and his sons, and also Kobi, are near the Kei, sometimes on one side, and sometimes on the other. The cattle taken from the Colony by Pato, Stock & Sandili, are this side the Kei and near the mouth. Pato says that he shall not make peace with the English, unless they give him back his country.

The Governor has given Stock eight days to restore the cattle stolen from Newtondale. In failing to do this he will be treated as an enemy.

October 31st: Some Hottentots passed through this morning from the Kat River to Waterloo Bay. They report having fallen in with some Kafirs, killing 4 of them, and capturing

7 horses. Stock sent in 20 cattle for those stolen from Newtondale. Capt. Maclean refused to accept them, stating that the Governor required the identical cattle.

November 2nd: From some Fingoes who have come from Jan Tshatshu's people, we learn that there is a large party of Fingoes near Butterworth anxious to come out if they could secure help.[63] They bid defiance to Rili. They state also that nearly all of Jan's people have been engaged in the war, and that they were present at the attack on Fort Peddie, though Jan was not himself. Some prisoners arrived from Newtondale. They stated that they were going to their old master at Oliphant's Hoek.[64] They were ordered off the Settlement, and threatened with the consequences if they were caught again.

Stock sent in 19 cattle, 3 horses, and 2 guns as the full remainder of colonial property & guns in his tribe. They also wished to know in what light Stock was considered by the Government, and stated that 3 of his men had been killed by Nonibi's people, and that he had no place to plough. Capt. Maclean answered that he only received the cattle &c as an instalment, and again reminded Stock that the Governor required the identical cattle stolen from Newtondale within the 8 days given him, or he must take the consequences.

Soon after 2 of Nonibi's women came to thank for the Governor's word, and to state that she accepted of his proposals of peace. Capt. Maclean sent word that she must bring the guns and stolen cattle, and that till she did that, all her professions would go for nothing. They denied what Stock's men said about their people having killed 3 of his men. In the afternoon Jan Tshatshu arrived with several followers. He stated that he came because he had understood from Mr. Brownlee that the Governor had sent for him. He behaved with the coolest effrontery imaginable, and wondered that other people should think and speak for him, when he had not done so himself. On being asked if he had any communication for the Government, he stated that he had none. He

was sent for. On this Capt. Maclean ordered him off the Post.
November 4th : Five of Umgai's women came to the Post last evening. They came to inform the Government that Umgai's children were returning to their country, and that they were now at the Keiskamma. Capt. Maclean sent them off with the information that if they ventured to return, a patrole should be sent out and they would be shot, and that when Umgai had a place for them, his children should be sent for.

Three Kafir girls arrived on the station, whom I sent over to Capt. Maclean, who ordered them off the Post.

November 6th : From a Fingoe who has fled hither from the Kafirs we learn that Umhala is wandering about with only 2 followers. He is afraid to trust himself with more. His councillors have proposed to him the plan of seizing Pato, and delivering him up to the Governor. They say he was the first to begin the war, and therefore he ought to be the first given up to the Government. Umhala however is afraid to act upon this plan at present. The Fingoe further says that Stock has been communicating with Umgai's & Pato's people, and encouraging them to come over to him, telling them that he had made peace, and was safe from the troops. Stock had also received some horses from the Gaikas to hide away from Sandili, lest he should give them up to the Governor. An express arrived from Beaufort. The Governor had given Maqomo 6 days, and Sandili 14 days, to bring in their guns & the captured cattle & horses.[65]

This is the last of the 8 days given to Stock for bringing in the cattle stolen from Newtondale. They have not made their appearance, and consequently Stock ought again to be considered as an enemy.

November 11th : Yesterday a party of Fingoes went to a part of the Fish River Bush, near Piet Apple tower, in order to see if there were still any of the goods there, plundered from the wagons which were burnt on the 21st May last.[66] They found nothing, however, of any consequence, neither did they see any traces of Kafirs.

Stock sent in some cattle for the Government to retain till he can restore those stolen from Newtondale. He pretends to have some difficulty with Nonibi about them. Capt. Maclean refused to receive them.

Jack's[67] wife and another woman came in last night, but they were immediately ordered off.

November 12th : An express came in from Col. Somerset and from Newtondale to say that Kafirs, or the spoer of Kafirs, had been seen going into the Colony.

November 13th : Some Kafirs were about the Settlement last night trying to get off some cattle, but in this they did not succeed. Umgai's people are said also to have returned to their places with fine herds of cattle, and information has been sent off to Col. Somerset to this effect.[68]

Some of Jan Tshatshu's people brought in Mr. Brownlee's horse and a side-saddle. They hold out some prospect, also, that he may be able to get out a few oxen and cows left from his stock, and also other things. They state that Jan did not go to the Governor when he left this, but to Sandili; and that Sandili is busy in collecting cattle and guns from his people, Jan's being required to give up their quota.

November 14th : Some Fingoes, who had been sent out as spies, returned this morning with the information that there were several Kafir kraals along the Gwanga with cattle. They came upon one before they were aware, and saw some Kafir men asleep under the kraal fence.

November 17th : Three women came in from Nonibi's to ask whether they were to bring in their guns here, or to give them up with Sandili's. Sandili had sent to her to give up some to him as her quota. They were told that such a message could only be considered as an evasion. If they intended to give up their guns, they must do so here. They were then ordered off. Stock has removed to the country about the Igqibira.

November 19th : Col. Somerset's division passed through to-day into Kafirland. They encamped for the night near our

Kafirs on the edge of the Bush

Beka Station, and we took the opportunity of riding over to see the premises. The destruction of the house is more complete than I expected. Every thing combustible is burnt except a door or two, and the walls are a good deal broken. The walls of the chapel are nearly entire. I picked up a Catechism on the Christian Religion in the garden, which is the only book I left that escaped the flames. We found also the bell, which I had brought away.

November 21st: Nonibi sent in 1 horse, 2 guns, and 13 cattle, some of the latter being those which we sent to meet Mr. Green last March,[69] and which were stolen from the man. Capt. M. rejected them, and ordered all off forthwith.

Col. Somerset went out yesterday on a patrole from the Beka. To-day he went to meet Capt. Hogg, who is now encamped at the Gwanga. They both move off to-morrow on a combined patrol across the Keiskamma.

From Stock's men Umzaya & Pai we learn that when Stock sent to ask Pato why he had joined in the war, Pato replied that Xosa had led him into it by attacking the Fingoes at Newtondale. They say also that Xala, a man whom Stock had not long before made an Umpakati,[70] began the war by sheltering the thieves of Rili's tribe, thus showing that Rili's people were engaged in the war from the very commencement.

Report saith that Mr. Calderwood has been appointed Civil Commissioner for the Gaikas at £500 a year![71]

Also that the Gaikas are busy in returning cattle, horses, & guns, and in fact bid fair to come up to something like the mark. And that the murderers of the Hottentot & those who fell on the Escort,[72] have been given up in whole or in part. All this moreover is attributed to Jan Tshatshu's exertions. The whole, however, wants confirmation.

November 23rd: Some horse and mule wagons arrived this morning with supplies for Col. Somerset's division. They proceed to his camp to-morrow. Firing has been heard nearly all day, and several kraals seen on fire, in the direction of the Keiskamma and Tamara.

It seems that the Governor gave the Gaikas five additional days, in order that any peaceably disposed persons might give themselves up, to be enrolled and located for the present at Lovedale. Maqomo not being able to get his people to submit, has given himself up unconditionally.

November 24th : The mule & horse wagons started for Col. Somerset's camp this morning. On reaching the Keiskamma heights, two burghers were sent on to reconnoitre the path. They saw two mounted Kafirs, and afterwards more Kafirs and cattle in the bush. As they had a small escort it was thought most prudent to return hither, and which they accordingly did. They heard a good deal of firing, both cannon and musketry.

November 25th : Col. Somerset has reported the capture of about 2 000 head of cattle, and killing 13 Kafirs, amongst Nonibi's people. He lost 2 of the Cape corps. Messengers had come to him from Umhala, Stock, Nonibi & Siyolo, & it is said that about 40 men had come in to lay down their arms. He has located Umkye's wives near the Keiskamma.

The news from the Governor's camp does not appear satisfactory. He seems to have lost his firmness and decision in great part. It is said that he has extended the time of the armistice 10 days, and waived his demand for the cattle. The Gaika chiefs have given up each a bundle of assegais in token of submission to British authority. The murderer of the Hottentot prisoner had been also given up, as also the man that shot Capt. Norden[73] at the beginning of the war. Wrote to the Secretaries.

November 30th : The 6th Regt. and the Rifles[74] have passed through on their way to join Col. Somerset's division. The mule wagons have returned and gone again with more supplies. It appears that the two Cape corps were not killed in battle, but were waylaid and murdered near Siyolo's kraal, to which they were induced to go for milk by some women. Capt. Hogg's party have taken the captured cattle to Block drift.

December 1st: Capt. Maclean returned last night from the Governor's camp, and has received a similar appointment in relation to the Dhlambi[75] tribes, as Mr. Calderwood has in relation to the Gaikas. The salary is £500 a year, with £50 additional for travelling expenses, and £120 for a clerk. The general intelligence is far more satisfactory than we were led to suppose. His Excellency continues firm in his demands from the Kafirs, as conditions of peace. They are:
1st Surrender of fire-arms;
2nd Restoration of Colonial booty;
3rd Retirement from the immediate frontier to such more Eastern parts of the country on this side of the Kei river, as the Governor should assign to them, where they should live under subjection to the British Government.

Previous to the general submission the Governor has made arrangement for individual submission on the following terms:
Each one to deliver up his gun or 6 assegais; to be registered with his dependents; his cattle to be also registered; to receive a ticket entitling him as a British subject to live in British Kafirland.[76] The question of cattle is to be settled between the tribes as bodies and the Government. The Government will hereafter recognize no chieftainship in British Kafirland.[77] No Kafirs who had taken part in the war, could be permitted to locate themselves between the Keiskamma and the Colony, nor between the Tyumi[78] and the Colony. Between this line and the Kei, up to which the Governor had taken possession for the Queen of England, they may live subject to the Queen, wherever they please, where they will be free from molestation, so long as they conduct themselves justly and peaceably.

If any kraal or tribe in British Kafirland plunders the Colony or the ceded territory, the Troops will immediately march over and punish the offending tribe and take their cattle. No tribe must make war on another tribe under penalty of being driven over the Kei. It was not for their land the Governor made war, but to punish them for their insulting & plundering the colony.

The land taken from them is not for the white people, but will be allotted to coloured people, who will be more just and peaceable than the Kafirs.[79]

Maqomo has gone out of his mind in consequence, as supposed, of a stroke of the sun. The Kafir given up as the murderer of the Hottentot prisoner, died soon after his arrival probably of fright.

Jan Tshatshu has been convicted of eating up some of the native Christians who had fled across the Kei, in order to avoid joining in the war.

December 4th: Conway's[80] party of Fingoes passed through this morning with about 500 cows and calves which they had captured from Stock's people. Stock's brother Ngceleshe came in with three men, to see Maclean about them. They were sent off the post, and directed to Somerset's camp if they wished to see Maclean. Capt Maclean and Shepstone[81] started yesterday morning, and expect to be with the camp some time, in order to locate such friendly Kafirs as choose to submit to the Government.

December 5th: Mr. Brownlee returned last evening from Block Drift. A patrole had captured 1 500 head of cattle, and killed amongst others Sandili's head Councillor. Sandili had sent in word to say that they had cut off his right hand. Some of the cattle taken, were claimed by the Kafirs who had received tickets of location, but they were very properly refused to them. Numbers had come in since to be registered, but took care to bring in more cattle, upon which the Governor informed them, that if he did not get sufficient cattle from other quarters, he should come upon them for their share. It appears that Sandili after collecting cattle & guns professedly to give up to the Government, has divided them out amongst his principal chiefs & great men. This has made the Governor desirous of getting hold of Sandili's private property, in order to make him feel personally the bitter effects of war.

Our chapel at Newtondale was burnt a few days since, in consequence of some sparks falling on the roof during a heavy wind.

December 9th: Col. Somerset has been encamped the last few days at the Buffalo, near Mt. Coke, but had not done any thing on account of the rain. He was to have moved however last night upon Pato, whose cattle, it is understood, are all between the Nxarune and Rulu[82] rivers & near the coast.

Umhala had been into the camp twice with men, cattle, horses, & guns, but so few of either, that Col. Somerset had ordered him off on both occasions. Pato had been himself to Umhala, to ask his advice as to whether he should give himself up to the Government or not. Umhala advised him not to try the experiment. As Umhala left the camp the second time, his people stole a span of Lucas's oxen which were at work outside, and the leader was missing when Lucas wrote.[83]

December 14th: Returned this afternoon from Col. Somerset's camp at the Buffalo river, and whither I accompanied Mr. Shaw on the 10th inst. Col. Somerset returned on the 11th inst. from a patrole, having captured about 250 cattle and killed some of the enemy, and who are supposed to be Pato's people. On the same day Umhala came in and also two of Kobi's sisters with a message from Pato to ask for peace, and which Capt. M. referred to the Governor for an answer. Mr. Shaw had some conversation with both Umhala & the two women. On the 12th inst. Umhala came with upwards of 200 men, 141 of whom, including himself, were registered, each giving up a gun or 6 assegais in token of submission to the British Government. On Sunday Mr. Shaw preached to the English troops, and I to the Provisionals and Fingoes. At night a small patrole went out. Lucas's boy had returned and confessed that the oxen had been stolen by three of Umkye's men, so that Umhala is clear from the charge preferred against him. Some of Stock's & Umkye's men had also come in, and would probably be registered in a day or two. The Kafirs appeared to be thoroughly tired of war, and anxious for peace. They dread the idea of being driven across the Kei, and this perhaps more than any thing else will make them submit to the Government. Kobi's sisters deny that Pato issued the order for killing the Fingoes in his country.[84]

December 16th : Mr. Shaw left us this morning on his return home. Last evening he had some conversation with the burnt woman, and from her account there does not appear any proof that Pato published the decree alleged against him, that all Fingoes in his country should be killed. It seems more probable that the man was killed for the sake of getting his cattle by his master, and that the women might have escaped if they had not run into another house. A few Fingoes, principally Kaulela's[85] people, brought in this morning about 100 head of cattle which they had captured from Siyolo's people, just over the Keiskamma. One Kafir was killed, and a Fingoe slightly wounded in the arm.

December 19th : The patrole which left the camp on Sunday evening last has returned,[86] having captured 250 head of cattle, and killed a few Kafirs, at the mouth of the Jamjam. The whole camp are to move in a day or two for the Kei. About 500 men had been registered. Kobi's sisters had been driven off, it having been found out that they had not been sent by Pato, but they had come at the instigation of Kobi to act as well as they could. They did not appear to know where Pato was, and from the direction which they took, it was supposed that Kobi was at the mouth of the Buffalo. They had heard from a Fingoe that Pato had been fallen upon by Rili,[87] and had lost some of his men & cattle at the Kei drifts. Also that Pato was now this side of the Kei with a large number of men and cattle, and determined to make a stand against the Troops. Some of his people are said to be at the mouth of the Keiskamma. We have heard that part of the first division[88] commenced a forward movemen (sic) on the 15th inst.

1847

January 6th : For the last few days I have been laid up with fever and sore throat. Through the Divine blessing on the means employed, I am now nearly recovered.

By the latest news from England we learn that Sir H. Pottinger[89] is to supersede Sir P. Maitland in the Governorship of the Colony. He was to sail in the "Gladiator" about the 10th of Nov. last, and may therefore be daily expected.

The latest news from the army is that His Excellency and Col. Somerset had crossed the Kei, and that a patrole had captured upwards of 5 000 cattle, and killed 40 Kafirs, belonging to Kobi's tribe. A camp had been formed near Fort Warden,[90] and Col. Johnson was at King William's Town.

January 9th : Reports have reached us that the Troops have captured 2 000 head of cattle belonging to Pato in addition to the above, and that Pato himself had a narrow escape from being shot by Col. Somerset.[91] It is said that the troops will return to this side of the Kei, till the plans of our new Governor are made known.

January 30th : Returned from attending our District Meeting in Graham's Town last evening.[92] On our way from Waterloo Bay we fell in with some Kafirs near Newtondale, but we were mercifully preserved from harm, some wagons and Cape Corps being providentially only a short distance ahead of us. I am appointed to D'Urban, Fort Peddie, this year. Mr. Green goes to Cradock, and Mr. Holden to D'Urban, Port Natal. Other arrangements may yet be made in reference to this part of the country by a special District meeting, when the views of our New Governor, now daily expected, are made known.

The Kafirs are about in this neighbourhood again, and various rumours are afloat. It is said that Pato intends attacking Waterloo Bay, and that Sandili, Siyolo, Tola, and Sonto, have agreed to fall on the first patrol which enters their country.[93] The cattle taken over the Kei have been sent into the Colony, and Col. Somerset is falling back to the Buffalo, to refresh his horses and men. The Registering system appears to have had no good effect generally. Capt. Maclean has returned, having only registered 800 men. Mr. Calderwood has registered 3 000, but in several cases he has been content to receive 1 assegai in token of submission. In fact we seem to be just as far from peace now, as when that system commenced.

February 8th : Col. Somerset has arrived at Fort Peddie, which now becomes the Head Quarters of the Cape Corps, and the 6th Regt. About 1 200 men are left at King William's Town, and posts are to be formed at Breakfast Vleij and at the Tua river, whilst Newtondale & Trumpetter's are to be strengthened. Our New Governor has arrived at Cape Town,[94] and has sent word to Col. Somerset to proceed with Sir Peregrine's plans till he comes up.

February 21st : Mr. Green and family left for Cradock early this morning. May the Lord be with them in all their journeyings, and bring them in peace and safety to the place of their destination!

The new Governor has sailed from Cape Town, and is daily expected in Graham's Town.[95] Col. Somerset is at Block Drift. Every thing appears to be in a state of suspense. Nothing is doing on our side, and yet the Kafirs are again troubling the Colony, and are also about in this neighbourhood. May the Lord arise in our behalf, and quickly subdue our enemies!

March 3rd : The Hon. Sir H. Pottinger, our New Governor, and Lieut. Gen. Sir Geo. Berkely,[96] Commander of the forces, have arrived in Graham's Town. Little has transpired as yet with regard to their intentions. It is rumoured however that Sir Henry is determined to have no half-measures, and that he will require the demand made upon the Kafirs to be fully paid. It is also said that a forward move into Kafirland is take place about the 16th or 18th of this month. It is time that something was done, for nothing can be more unsatisfactory than the present aspect of affairs. May the Lord give wisdom and discretion to our new rulers!

March 16th: Sir Geo. Berkely arrived a few days since at Fort Peddie, and preparations appear to be making for a forward movement. The Burgher force has been invited by the Governor to take the field of their own free will, and thus prevent the necessity of proclaiming Martial law.[97] On Saturday last 57 oxen were carried off the Settlement by Kafirs, but were soon retaken by the Fingoes. Yesterday morning it was discovered that a drove of cattle had passed by in the preceding night, which were traced into Nonibi's country. In the afternoon 3 spans of oxen were captured by the ever watchful enemy, who succeeded in carrying them clear off.

On Sunday Col. Michel[98] of the 6th R. had the garrison at Fort Peddie marched for divine service to our Station chapel, a great improvement on our previous arrangements. I hope this may be continued.

March 22nd: The Governor and suite arrived last Friday evening. It is said that some move is to take place immediately, but nothing is publicly known with any certainty. Despatches were received from the Gaika District, stating that the Gaikas were for peace. Sandili had determined to have no more war,[99] and had said that those of his people who would not submit, must leave the country.

Several burghers from Albany and Uitenhage have arrived, ready to take the field with the Troops.[100]

Yesterday afternoon Sir Harry & suite attended Divine service with the Peddie Garrison at our Station chapel.

March 25th: The troops left this morning for the Tua where they will form a post, and thence proceed into Kafirland. The General has gone with them but the Governor remains here for the present.

Pato has sent in to surrender. The Governor has sent him word back that he must surrender unconditionally, but that his life shall be preserved.[101]

April 2nd: Col. Somerset's party have captured about 200 cattle & killed 4 or 5 Kafirs. Capt. Maclean & W. Shepstone started for the Buffalo on Sunday last. The 73rd have moved down there from King William's Town to form a post. A post has been formed at Wesleyville[102] and not at the Tua. The troops have moved on to the Buffalo.

On Wednesday evening the Kafirs took 5 spans of oxen from R. Tainton's convoy of wagons, as they were outspanned on the flat below our Beka station. Some men went from here to assist in recovering them, but they arrived too late to be of any service.

April 13th: Sixth Anniversary of wedding day. Held a Missionary meeting in our Fingoe chapel. Good congregation though composed principally of women and children, most of our men being in the field with the Troops. Collection £7. 8s. 7d. – A noble one under all the circumstances of the case.

Our troops are encamped along the Buffalo in different positions, and keep patroling the country but with little effect. Two burghers have been killed, and two or three of the 6th have been wounded on escort duty. Major Smith[103] of the 73rd has been badly wounded in the arm. Col. Somerset was to have started yesterday or to-day towards the mouth of the Kei, in which neighbourhood Pato is supposed to be. His cattle are still over the Kei.

April 26th: Sir Geo. Young,[104] our New Lieut. Governor, arrived last night at Peddie to see His Excellency Sir Henry Pottinger. This evening he came over to the Station, and I walked with him to the Post. He seems interested in Missionary operations. Affairs remain in statu quo, nothing of any importance having occurred lately.

May 29th: Nothing has occurred during the course of this month of much importance. Both the Governor and the General are here, and from all appearances intend to remain for the winter. We have made a commencement in setting our Mission premises in repair.

October 26th: About a month since our troops again took the field, after lying still during the winter. They commenced operations against the Gaikas, burning out their country, and sweeping through the Amatolas. A few of the enemy have fallen, and some three or four thousand cattle have been captured. Sandili has given himself up,[105] and passed here a day or two since on his way to the Governor, who is now in Graham's Town.

By the late English papers we learn that we are to have another change of Governors. Sir H. Pottinger is to be Governor of Madras, and to be succeeded here by Sir Harry Smith,[106] who was here during the last Kafir war, and may be supposed therefore to know something of the Kafirs.

Mr. Stirk[107] had a narrow escape from the Kafirs yesterday. He was out cutting forage some distance from the Post, when towards evening he was accosted by a mounted Kafir who knew him, and told him not to be afraid, as he would do him no harm, but that he was hungry, and wanted meat. Soon afterwards two others made their appearance, and Mr. S. thought it was time to run. There were eight altogether, & all mounted on good horses. They were Pato's people, and of course made off with the oxen, & such other things as they could lay hands upon. This is the first instance perhaps in which the Kafirs have spared the life of an Englishman during this war, and is a most wonderful interposition of Divine providence on behalf of Mr. S. which I trust will not be lost on him.

Last Sunday I had the pleasure of baptizing seven adults of the Fingoe nation, and admitting them into the Christian church. I preached in Kafir from the Ethiopian eunuch,[108] which was the first time of my preaching in Kafir in the forenoon service. I had done so previously only in our early morning services.

November 22nd: Returned on Saturday from Waterloo Bay where we spent the preceeding Sabbath. The Fingoe congregation amounted to about 150, most of whom were clean and dressed in European fashion. The English congregation in the evening was small. Col. Somerset has had lately two engagements with the Kafirs near the Kei river. Several of the enemy were killed or wounded, and some horses, guns, &c. captured. The General has joined Col. Somerset with the intention of crossing over together into Rili's country. Sad intelligence reached us a few days since, of the death of 5 Officers who had imprudently left the camp to view the neighbouring country, by the hands of Kafirs, who seem to have fallen upon them unawares, and barbarously mutilated them.[109]

December 24th : During the last few days important changes have taken place in the political affairs of this country. Sir H. Pottinger & Sir George Berkely have left the frontier, and our new Governor, Sir Harry Smith, has arrived among us.[110] He has already issued a proclamation[111] in virtue of which, the ceded territory & upwards to the Orange river, becomes part & parcel of the Cape Colony. On Wednesday last I rode to King William's Town, where I met with Mr. Shaw & Mr. Impey. On Thursday the Governor arrived & held a meeting with all the Kafir chiefs,[112] including Pato who had just surrendered to Col. Somerset, in which he received their submission, and announced the termination of hostilities. Thus after nearly two years' war, we are again permitted to see the return of peace, which I trust will be permanently and satisfactorily established. Another meeting is to be held on the 7th of January next, when the chiefs will receive their different locations and commissions, in compliance with the new arrangements. The country between the Keiskamma & the Kei is to be called British Kaffraria, and to be under the entire control of the British government, though not as yet intended to be included in the Colony.[113] The new district just included in the Colony, is to be termed Victoria.[114] Waterloo Bay is to be called Fort Albert.

Notes and References

1. Unidentified.
2. A London Missionary Society station in Lower Albany, founded in 1813.
3. Provisionals or levies.
4. Unidentified.
5. Fort Dacres consisted largely of earthworks and acted as a commissariat store for a few months. Its purpose was to protect a pont which was put on the river as part of a new route to Fort Peddie, but it was soon superseded by Waterloo Bay (See below p. 93) G. E. Cory *Rise of South Africa* Vol. IV p. 463.
6. Unidentified.
7. There was little else he could do before some measure of peace was restored.
8. The Irura has not been identified.
9. Maitland's return of troops of a fortnight later shows the number of regular troops in the Colony as 3,049, native levies as 4,313 and burghers 9,308. PP 786 p. 177.
10. Capt. W. Hogg, ? –1852, of the 7th Dragoon Guards, commanded a native levy.
11. Two months later Maitland complained to Secretary of State Gladstone that the drought had made him feel insecure "in every position"; and that the tactics of the Kafirs contributed to reducing his war effort to "skirmishes and occasional captures of cattle . . ." He had no other tactics. Maitland to Gladstone, 18 September 1846, PP 786, p. 154.
12. The Jamjam has not been identified.
13. Unidentified.
14. or Rili.
15. i.e. Committee's Drift Post.
16. cf. above, p. 45.
17. Lt. Col. M. Johnstone.
18. The Green River is a tributary of the Buffalo which originates between King William's Town and the Debi flats.
19. The Debi flats lie to the west of King William's Town and south of the Amatola mountains.
20. This was more of a threat than a promise. Maitland was not convinced of Sirili's guilt. Maitland to Gladstone, 18 September 1846. PP 786 p. 156.
21. The Gqunubi river lies to the east of the Buffalo river and East London.
22. King William's Town had been established in 1835 by Sir Benjamin D'Urban and was Lt.-Col. Harry Smith's headquarters from which he controlled Queen Adelaide Province.
23. Rev. John Brownlee, of the London Missionary Society, stationed on the Buffalo next to the military buildings of King William's Town.
24. Tshatshu or Tzatzoe had achieved notoriety on the Frontier when he was taken to England by Dr. Philip in 1836 as an example of the success of the London Society's work. He was a minor chief and mission teacher who lived within two miles of King William's Town. According to Cory, Jan Tshatshu was excommunicated by Brownlee for his part in this war. *Rise of South Africa* Vol. IV p. 452.
25. *Wrongs of the Caffre Nation* by "Justus", (pseud. for M. Beverley) London, 1837. This controversial book, often mistakenly attributed to Dr. Philip, took the view that the Xosa had suffered unjustly in the war of 1834–5.
26. Capt. C. L. Maitland, one of the Governor's sons.
27. Faku, chief of the Pondo tribe, situated to the north-east of Sirili's Gcalekas and in treaty relationship with Britain since 1843. This report was merely a rumour and Faku was not involved in the war. The Bashee is the next large river to the north-east of the Kei.

[28] Captain Sir Harry Darell, 1814-53, who was wounded at the battle of the Gwanga.
[29] Fort Beresford was situated to the north of King William's Town near the source of the Buffalo river.
[30] Fort Cox was established in 1835 and named after Major W. Cox of the 75th Regiment. It lay in the Amatolas and featured prominently in the following war. See below pp. 122, 123, 125.
[31] The burning of grass in winter was common practice but this seems to have been a scorched-earth strategy.
[32] The Tsomo is a tributary of the Kei which flows through what was Gcaleka territory.
[33] Negotiations for Stock's surrender extended over another five days (see above p. 91) but the final date is still about five days earlier than that given by Cory. G. E. Cory *Rise of South Africa* Vol. IV p. 499.
[34] Clauses 2 and 3 are a recapitulation of Sir Benjamin D'Urban's extreme position of May 1835, and equally impractical. See W. M. Macmillan *Bantu, Boer and Briton* p. 154. Actually Maitland had no definite settlement in view and his treatment of Stock makes this clear.
[35] Maitland does not seem to have believed this. In his dispatch to Gladstone, 18 September 1846, he states that Stock might originally have been "forced into hostilities". PP. 786 p. 156.
[36] See above p. 59.
[37] See above, p. 65.
[38] The Kwelera river lies about half way between the Buffalo and the Kei.
[39] See above, p. 92.
[40] It is interesting to speculate on how Appleyard knew this.
[41] According to W. M. Macmillan, Stockenstrom wanted to "get Kreli's sanction for annexation up to the Kei River by a treaty, such as they now lacked, for compelling him to do his share in keeping the Ciskeian tribes in order." *Bantu, Boer and Briton* p. 294.
[42] Unidentified.
[43] Jabez Aldum was killed and his body mutilated on 3 August. Mapoma, Mapassa's brother, was held responsible.
[44] See above, p. 62.
[45] Maitland did not assent to Stockenstrom's "treaty" as he suspected Sirili of "usual Kafir duplicity". He refused to "recognise in him any right whatever to dispose of the territories west of the Kei", and insisted on the restoration of colonial cattle by Sirili as a condition of peace. Maitland to Gladstone 18 September 1846. PP 786 p. 156.
[46] Waterloo Bay was the name given to a small bay about a mile east of the Fish River mouth. The schooner *Waterloo* successfully unloaded cargo there and it was hoped to be able to provision Fort Peddie from there, but it was soon abandoned in favour of the Buffalo mouth. G. E. Cory *Rise of South Africa* Vol. IV pp. 463 & 496.
[47] The Nxarune river is probably the "Kahoon" or Nahoon which flows through part of East London.
[48] The Nyulusi river is probably that marked "Umnulutzi" on Mr. Donald's map. It is an eastward-flowing tributary of the Keiskama.
[49] The memorandum with which Shaw supplied Maitland is contained in Maitland to Grey, 14 October 1846. PP 786 p. 188-89. It is dated "camp at the Fish River mouth", 16 September.
[50] Mozambiquers, presumably negroid ex-slaves, originally from Mocambique, who had migrated into the area. For the term see J. S. Marais, *Cape Coloured People*, 1652-1937, p. 1 and note.

⁵¹ Already Maitland has accepted significant modifications to the plan announced to Stock. See above, p. 90.
⁵² Hare died on his voyage to England in September 1846. Lt.-Col. Johnstone succeeded to his military but not to his civil position.
⁵³ Hermanus was the leader of a band of Xosas and featured prominently in the next war as an enemy of the colonists. See below, pp. 126 & 127.
⁵⁴ The influence of the various missionary societies on Maitland at this time was considerable. Shaw's power of acting within the area assigned to him, was great. He took the initiative in January 1847 in inviting another group of Fingoes, who had remained in Gcaleka territory, to stay near Fort Peddie while he prepared fresh locations for them. In this connection his power within the Wesleyan Society as General Secretary was also demonstrated:
 "If requisite I will appoint one or two of the Missionaries to be on the spot and take temporary charge of these people, till all the arrangements for their final location can be completed . . ."
W. Shaw to Colonial Secretary, Fort Beaufort 2 January 1847. Cape Archives, C.O. 565.
⁵⁵ Rev. H. Calderwood, 1808?–1865, of the London Missionary Society, in 1845 had established the Birklands mission (now Healdtown).
⁵⁶ It is not known on what terms Appleyard obtained these supplies. Presumably while at Fort Peddie the missionaries had received rations from the commissariat and on leaving the Fort had to find all their own necessities in unfavourable circumstances: most wagons would have been commandeered by the military.
⁵⁷ The Kwelera is so close to the Gqunubi that it is difficult to understand from Appleyard's text why Somerset did not take some action to verify the report.
⁵⁸ Negotiations had begun as a result of overtures from the Gaikas themselves. Makomo had approached Lt.-Col. Campbell (see above, p. 30 – Major Campbell) at Fort Cox on behalf of all the Gaika chiefs to ask for peace. On 30 September Lt.-Col. Johnstone, accompanied by Major Smith the frontier commissioner, Rev. Calderwood and Rev. Kayser, met Makomo, Sandili, Botman, Tola, some minor chiefs and hundreds of tribesmen near Lovedale. The Governor's demands were the restoration of all stolen cattle, the surrender of all guns and the location of the Gaikas in another place under British rule. Sandili and Botman rejected the terms outright and were especially vehement about not parting with their guns. Sandili insisted however that he would sow and not fight. What the Gaikas wanted was an armistice and not a settlement. G. E. Cory *Rise of South Africa* Vol. IV pp. 499–501.
⁵⁹ Makomo's submission was personal and Sandili did not follow his example. See above, p. 102.
⁶⁰ The Tua river is probably that marked "Tooi" on Mr. Donald's map of Peddie. It flows in an easterly direction into the Keiskama.
⁶¹ The Shushu river flows in a westerly direction into the Keiskama.
⁶² It is not known to what the "blunder" refers.
⁶³ See above, footnote 54.
⁶⁴ Oliphant's Hoek lies on the Fish river a few miles north-east of Committees Drift. Map by James Wyld, *Graham's Town and the Out Posts*.
⁶⁵ Sandili did not meet the demand and when the 14 days expired Maitland was not unduly concerned. He believed that he could circumvent the chief and that Sandili's people would soon submit. Maitland to Grey, 26 November 1846. PP. 786 p. 194.
⁶⁶ See above, p. 59.
⁶⁷ There is a "Jack" mentioned in the Return of Passes granted to Fingoes at Fort Peddie in November 1841, but this does not constitute identification. Cape Archives, L.G. 408 p. 55.

⁶⁸ Maitland described this period as one in which the two sides were "neither at war nor at peace". Maitland to Grey, 26 November 1846. PP. 786 p. 195.
⁶⁹ Not mentioned previously. Presumably they were sent to help Green reach safety at Fort Peddie or the D'Urban station.
⁷⁰ i.e. counsellor. According to the *Christian Watchman*, Vol. I 1846, p. 398, the "Amapakati" (plural) were "middle ones" between the chief and tribesmen, and had some civil jurisdiction.
⁷¹ See above, p. 103. Calderwood states that he agreed to become commissioner for the Gaikas only on condition that Maitland gave up his intention of driving them out of the Amatolas. H. Calderwood, *Caffres and Caffre Missions*, p. 52.
⁷² The killer and the original thief were given up by Sandili on 4 November 1846. J. E. M. Verwey *Oorlog van die Byl: die Sewende Kafferoorlog, 1846–48*, M.A. thesis, unpublished; University of Stellenbosch, 1955, p. 144.
⁷³ J. D. Norden, 1803 ?–25 April 1846, commander of the Graham's Town Yeomanry. He was shot in the head and his body mutilated.
⁷⁴ i.e. Cape Mounted Rifles.
⁷⁵ i.e. Ndhlambi.
⁷⁶ "British Kafirland" was to be the land between the Tyumie-Keiskama line and the Kei.
⁷⁷ This is correct. Maitland to Grey, 26 November 1846, PP. 786 p. 196. Maitland aimed to substitute another system of control for that of the chiefs. Villages or kraals were to be placed under "steady and intelligent" tribesmen who would act as headmen, having constabulary powers; groups of villages were to fall under superior headmen, who might coincidentally be the old councillors or chiefs; and there were to be commissioners or magistrates with each group of tribes, such as the Gaikas and Ndhlambis. The commissioners were to have far more authority than those of the Glenelg-Stockenstrom Treaty System, and their control was to be real.

Maitland tried also to treat the Xosa tribesmen as individually guilty or not guilty of involvement in hostilities against the Colony. Both his new pattern of authority and his idea of individual responsibility failed in practice.
⁷⁸ The Tyumie or Chumie is the largest tributary of the Keiskama and rises in the Amatolas.
⁷⁹ cf. above, p. 94.
⁸⁰ M. Conway, 1813– ?, of Graham's Town.
⁸¹ W. G. B. Shepstone, who had become Maclean's unpaid assistant. Gordon, R. E. *Shepstone*, p. 73.
⁸² The Rulu river has not been identified.
⁸³ This is Appleyard's only reference to information on the war being supplied to him by a correspondent. The information itself is almost amusing. See below p. 144 for correction.
⁸⁴ See above, p. 52.
⁸⁵ Kaulela was one of the Fingoe chiefs. J. Ayliff and J. Whiteside *History of the Abambo (Fingos)* p. 40.
⁸⁶ See above, p. 105.
⁸⁷ No large-scale attack was made by Sirili on Pato, but Pato was in fear of Sirili's capturing him.
⁸⁸ Commanded by Lt.-Col. Johnstone.
⁸⁹ Sir Henry Pottinger, 1789–1856, Governor of the Cape, 27 January–1 December 1847. Left to become Governor of Madras, a task at which he was not successful.
⁹⁰ Fort Warden was situated on the road from King William's Town to the Kei, and near the Kei.
⁹¹ This report is not substantiated.

⁹² The District Meeting began on 13 January 1847. Appleyard was appointed to D'Urban, but no thorough-going arrangements were made owing to the fact that the new Governor, Pottinger, might change Maitland's dispositions of the tribes. The missionaries would have to follow the people to whom they were assigned. The Minutes of the next annual District Meeting show that Appleyard spent at least the latter part of the year at Newtondale, together with Rev. J. Ayliff. See also Shaw's letter, quoted in note 54 above. The D'Urban station was the only one to be repaired in 1847.
⁹³ Appleyard probably obtained this information from Capt. Maclean. See G. E. Cory, *Rise of South Africa* Vol. V, p. 4-5.
⁹⁴ Pottinger arrived in Cape Town on 27 January 1847 and took the oaths of office on that day.
⁹⁵ He arrived at Port Elizabeth on 19 February and Graham's Town on 28 February 1847.
⁹⁶ Lieut.-General Sir George Berkeley, Commander-in-Chief of H.M. forces at the Cape. He arrived and departed with Pottinger.
⁹⁷ The declaration of martial law was avoided because, according to Pottinger's Proclamation of 3 March, he wished to avoid causing inconvenience to the civilian population. For the result, see below, note 100. Cory, *Rise of South Africa* Vol. V. p. 11.
⁹⁸ Lt.-Col. C. C. Michel, 1793-1851, a man of wide military experience and superintendent of works at the Cape 1828-48. Commander of Fort Peddie at this time.
⁹⁹ He said as much in a meeting which he had with Calderwood. G. E. Cory, *Rise of South Africa* Vol. V p. 9.
¹⁰⁰ The burger forces had been disbanded by Maitland in September 1846, after much friction between the burgher and regular forces. He had attempted a second draft within a month, but even after an offer of remuneration response was very poor. Maitland to Grey 18 September and 14 October 1846. PP. 786 p. 153 & 181.

Pottinger was faced with insufficient numbers of troops for his purposes. By Pottinger's Proclamation of 3 March 1847 burgher volunteers were promised that they should not be detained for more than one month in the field. This led to an unsatisfactory state of affairs. See G. E. Cory *Rise of South Africa* Vol. V pp. 32 & 33.
¹⁰¹ Pato did not accept the offer.
¹⁰² Fort Wellington, one of seven forts created by Pottinger.
¹⁰³ Major Smith may be T. C. Smith, who was in command of a section of 27th Regt. in Natal and subsequently Frontier Commissioner. See above, p. 13 note 45 & 46. For the above incident, see Cory, *Rise of South Africa*, Vol. V p. 31.
¹⁰⁴ Sir Henry E. F. Young, 1808-70, lieutenant governor of the Eastern Province, arrived at Port Elizabeth on 20 April 1847 and left on 3 November 1847.
¹⁰⁵ On 19 October 1847 Sandili had accompanied Capt. J. J. Bisset to Keiskama Hoek and thence to King William's Town and Fort Peddie en route to Graham's Town. There was considerable controversy as to the terms of his surrender and Capt. Maclean believed that Sandili had been cheated into unconditional surrender. Pottinger supported Maclean's view. G. E. Cory *Rise of South Africa* Vol. V pp. 44-48.

At Fort Peddie Sandili was incarcerated in the guard room for the night. Mr. J. M. Donald, Supplement to *Daily Dispatch*, 5 September 1960.
¹⁰⁶ Sir H. G. W. Smith, 1787-1860, victor of Aliwal, previously at the Cape from 1829-40. He administered the Province of Queen Adelaide for Sir Benjamin D'Urban in 1836 and founded King William's Town. Governor of the Cape, 1 December 1847-31 March 1852.

[107] Probably Joseph Stirk, 1802-1881, an immigrant of 1820 and later Divisional Councillor of Peddie. E. Morse Jones *Roll of the British Settlers* p. 158. Also photograph.
[108] See *Acts of the Apostles*, chapter 8 vv. 26-40.
[109] On 13 November 1847 Capt. Baker, Lt. Faunt, Ensign Burnop, Dr. Campbell and Asst. Surgeon Loch were killed.
[110] Pottinger left Graham's Town for Cape Town on 8 December 1847 and Smith arrived in Graham's Town on 17 December, when he liberated Sandili.
[111] The proclamation was dated 17 December 1847.
[112] On 23 December. Pato had surrendered on 19 December.
[113] This was similar to D'Urban's and to Maitland's schemes. British Kaffraria was to be divided into five "counties".
[114] i.e. the old Ceded or Neutral Territory. The capital of this district was to be not Fort Peddie but the new town of Alice. This was indicative of the change in strategic emphasis on the frontier: Alice was well placed to cover the Amatolas. See G. E. Cory *Rise of South Africa* Vol. V p. 104-05.

Introduction to Chapter V

The last chapter spans nearly 12 years. During this period Appleyard became increasingly occupied with the translating into Xosa of the Scriptures, and the printing of the whole Bible. He says too little about his work, and lengthy footnoting has been resorted to in order to establish its importance. An Appendix has been added to demonstrate the range of work which he and his two assistants in the printing establishment covered in the year in which they published the Bible in Xosa.

Life on the Frontier was changing. Sir Harry Smith came as Pottinger's successor to stamp on the embers of the War of the Axe. About two years later another and far more serious war was raging. Many of the Gaika chiefs and their subjects were restless under the burden of Smith's regime. Umlangeni, a war prophet, became the symbol of Xosa resistance to the white man. Hottentots also found the idea of sovereign independence alluring: on the outbreak of hostilities at the end of 1850 some of the rank and file of the Cape Mounted Rifles deserted to the Gaikas. The Gaikas, furthermore, were better organised than before, with more guns and greater accuracy of fire. Sir Harry Smith himself was besieged in Fort Cox and had to escape in disguise at the head of a large number of Mounted Riflemen, to King William's Town.

Three or four years after this struggle had ended, there was another, more hysterical, national prophecy of final victory over the oppressor. The preparations, during 1856 and 1857, for this Armageddon, resulted in the death or displacement through famine of about a third of all the tribes west of the Fish River. This is what we know as the Cattle Killing or national Suicide of the Ama-Xosa.

Appleyard was at the centre of the Umlageni war at its inception. His comments, though of their usual high quality, are not of the same rarity value as those which he had written at Fort Peddie.

Chapter V

Umlangeni, and the Bible in Xosa

1848

January 10th: On the 7th inst. I attended the meeting between the Governor and Kafirs, at which peace was formally concluded. Messrs. Shaw, Dugmore,[1] Pearse,[2] Impey & Warner,[3] were also there, as well as several Missionaries of other societies. The Governor sent for us after the meeting, and requested us to commence operations immediately, assuring us of his countenance and support. Messrs. Shaw, Dugmore, & Pearse, spent the Sabbath with us, and left for Waterloo Bay, this morning.

February 16th: Returned on Saturday evening last from attending our District meeting at Graham's Town.[4] Found Bro. Davis just arrived from Natal. I am appointed to Wesleyville which is now in British Kaffraria, but am not to remove thither till April. In the mean time, I can get some sort of a place ready, to serve for a house, till the Mission premises are erected. A dreadful flood occurred during my absence. The rain continued for 5 days & nights with very little intermission. On the fourth day the gable end of the chapel fell down, as did also two chimneys of the house.

November 7th: On March 1st last we left Fort Peddie to pay our long desired visit to Natal. As Mr. Shaw was about to proceed thither on official duty, it was thought better to postpone the re-establishment of Wesleyville till his return, so that our way seemed opened to do so. We accordingly proceeded to Algoa Bay, where we found the Curlew almost ready to sail. We embarked March 15th and landed at D'Urban on the 28th. Thence we proceeded to Pietermaritzburg, where Mr. Archbell was residing, and where we remained about 6 weeks.[5] We then returned to D'Urban, and took ship (the Douglas) for Algoa Bay, where we landed on May 31st thankful for all the mercies which we had received in all our journeyings and voyagings. Proceeding to Graham's Town, I found a letter from Mr. Shaw directing me to proceed to Bathurst, where we arrived June 24th, and where we have resided ever since. Our District meeting will take place shortly, when my future station will have to be decided. May my steps be directed from above! Wesleyville, I fear, will not be taken up at present, for want of men.

December 9th : Returned on the 7th inst. from attending our District meeting at Graham's Town.[6] It was a very delightful season. There is an increase of 235[7] members, besides upwards of 300 on trial. A verse of praise was sung in acknowledgement of God's goodness to us in this respect. I am appointed to King William's Town in charge of our Mission press. Bro. Jno. Smith succeeds me here, and Bro. Wilson[8] succeeds him at Port Elizabeth. Bro. Sargeant[9], who was ordained in Wesley chapel[10] Nov. 26th., is appointed to Wesleyville. I am to remain at Bathurst till Bro. Wilson is able to leave King William's Town, which will not be the case probably for five or six weeks.

1849

January 29th : We left Bathurst on the 9th instant, and arrived at King William's Town, British Kaffraria, on the 16th. We have now got tolerably settled in our new home.

February 4th : Preached morning and evening at East London, Buffalo Mouth. Small congregations.

February 11th : Took my turn at Fort Beaufort, where I preached morning and evening in the English chapel, and in the afternoon to the Fingoe congregation.

February 18th : Revd Mr. Thompson, of Graham's Town, preached for me this morning, and the Revd Mr. Dorrington, an Independent Minister recently arrived from England, in the evening.

December 23rd : To-day various presents were distributed to the Kafir chiefs & some of their principal men.[11]

December 24th : Our District Meeting has been held this year at Mt. Coke. Nineteen of us were present. We had a happy time.[12] All were of one heart and one mind. Bro. Pearse goes as Deputy Chairman to Natal, and it is hoped that he may be the means of restoring tranquillity to that part of the District. I remain here in charge of our Mission Press, which was removed hither last March.[13] Since that period I have been busy in attending to the printing of my work on the Kafir Language, which was happily completed just before our meeting.[14]

1850

December 29th : The year is closing upon us in eventful times.[15] The last few days have plunged us into another war with some of the Kafir tribes. Considerable disaffection has prevailed amongst them, particularly the Gaikas, for some time past. His Excellency Sir Harry Smith visited us here some two months back,[16] and endeavoured to remove it. He thought he had done so, and returned again to Cape Town. Hardly had he reached that place, however, before the disaffection broke out afresh, aggravated now by open resistance to British authority. Sir Harry immediately started again, and arrived here on the 9th inst. He summoned a meeting on the 14th of the Hlambi tribes who all promised to sit still. He explained to them that he had come up, not to make war, but to put down rebellion. Sandili, whom he had deprived of his chieftainship on the former visit, was now proclaimed a rebel and outlaw, and large rewards were offered for his capture as well as for that of "Anta", his brother, who with him had been the principal instigator of fomenting discontent and rebellion amongst the people.[17] On the 16th inst. one division of troops marched to the Kubusi,[18] and on the 17th another division marched to Fort Cox,[19] to which post His Excellency and Col. Mackinnon[20] also went on the following day. On Thursday the 19th a meeting of the Gaikas was called, and about 2500 were present. Their hearing was by no means satisfactory. These were also urged to sit still, as His Excellency only wanted to punish the guilty. Sutu, the mother of Sandili, was constituted chief in his place, and certain councillors were appointed for the Amambombo[21] tribe.

A patrol of 500 men under Col. Mackinnon left Fort Cox on Tuesday[22] to try and secure Sandili and Anta. After proceeding a few miles they were fired upon by a large party of Kafirs concealed in the bush through which they were marching. Some of the 6th Regt. were killed by the first shots of the treacherous enemy, as also the mules carrying the ammunition, which fell into their hands. For several hours constant firing was kept up on both sides, our troops falling back on Wednesday to Fort White,[23] where they arrived just in time to save it,[24] and then on to Fort Cox, where they are now encamped till levies can be brought from the Colony. The casualties on our side were 1 Officer (Surgeon) and 11 men killed, besides two officers and seven men wounded.[25]

Three of the 45th regt. were murdered last Tuesday on the high road between this and Fort Cox, and fourteen others on the following day, who had gone out from Fort White for the purpose of burying their comrades.[26]

We have been in a state of great excitement and alarm here since Xmas day, especially before the arrival of the Kubusi camp, which returned to us again on Friday evening.[27]

Last night we were alarmed by guns being fired off at some Kafirs who were trying to get some of the cattle away. Troops and Volunteers[28] all turned out, whilst the women and children went to places of safety. We are dreading an attack from the Kafirs. Our fears are considerably increased from the fact that some of the Cape corps are now in prison for mutiny, it being strongly suspected, also, that most of these men are ill-affected, and that they would join the Kafirs against us.[29] Three lighted coals were found in the thatch of the buildings in the Infantry barracks last night, and it is thought that they must have been put there with an evil purpose by some of them.

Intelligence reached us this morning that the post at Line drift was destroyed.[30] There were only a few of the Cape corps stationed there, who are supposed to have fled to Peddie.

December 30th: About the middle of last night we were roused by the sound of firing which appeared to be gradually approaching the town. We were soon relieved however by the arrival of about 20 men of the Cape Corps, who were returning from Fort White with the post. They had been fired upon by the Kafirs for some distance.

Several Missionaries have had some difficulty in retiring to places of safety. Mr. Niven and family[31] had to leave on horseback, [and after reaching the Tyumie station, had with others to fly to Fort Hare, protected by some military sent to their assistance by Col. Somerset.[32]] Mr. Niven's house was burnt as soon as he left, he and his station people losing all their property. Mrs. Brown[33] had to walk with her baby, and a single woman servant from the Igqibira to Fort White. Mr. MacDiarmid[34] fled to Fort Cox. Messrs. Ross,[35] Birt, and the Berlin Missionaries[36] have arrived here. Mr. White[37] got away with difficulty from Wesleyville, having been threatened by an armed party on their way to Mt. Coke. They escaped however through the interference of Dilima, who gave them an escort for their wagon, whilst he rode on with them to Mt. Coke, he carrying the children himself.[38] They arrived there all safe this afternoon. Mr. Impey intends to make a stand at Mt. Coke. He has been supplied with ammunition and guns from Fort Murray.[39]

Umhala and Siyolo have arranged to attack Fort Murray, so that the Hlambies have soon determined to break their faith.[40] I hope Pato will continue firm. Dilima is now at Ft. Murray with a few men for the purpose of fighting on our side. Jan Tshatshu is gone to stay at Ft. Murray. He cannot control his people. Most of them are disaffected.

Several of the Military settlers have been murdered – it is said as many as 47.⁴¹ Their wives and children were not killed.

One of the speakers at the late Gaika meeting who observed that "it was a pity that a whole country should be killed for one man" – has since been put to death. It is said also that Sutu and four of the Councillors appointed by the Governor, are also to be killed.⁴²

Fort Hare is reported to have been attacked, with considerable loss, however, to the Kafirs.⁴³

December 31st: The Governor and Col. Mackinnon arrived from Fort Cox, escorted by a large number of the Cape Corps.⁴⁴ They had to fight their way most of the distance. His Excellency seems in low spirits. His foolish boasting at the late meetings, prove how little he knew of the actual state of matters. The Kafirs are now masters of the field, and the Lord only can deliver us. May He speedily arise and help us!

A strong escort of the 91st proceeding from Fort Hare to Fort Cox with cattle and sheep were attacked on their way,⁴⁵ and lost 2 Officers and 21 men, besides a three-pounder gun, which they spiked and left behind.

A Scotchman⁴⁶ who had remained behind in Toise's⁴⁷ country, reached town safely to-day. Toise himself escorted him as far as Ft. Murray, but he had difficulty nevertheless in getting through. He describes the country as being black with Kafirs.

1851

January 1st: With the exception of the last two or three weeks, the year now past was one of much hope and encouragement with regard to our Mission work in this country. The labours of the Missionaries of different Societies were crowned with success, whilst a thirst for knowledge evidently existed amongst the converts. A Kafir and English newspaper was commenced last August, printed at our press, and had from the first a large circulation.⁴⁸ The new year, however, opens upon us with very different prospects. War is desolating the land. Missionaries and their flocks are again scattered. The heathen are raging around us. All, from the Governor downwards, appear to be paralysed. Yet we should not despair. "The Lord reigneth," and can bring us help and salvation. May we all call upon Him in this the day of our trouble!

January 2nd : The Burnshill Mission station has been burnt, as also Mr. Brownlee's house at Fort Cox.[49] Hermanus's Kafirs have risen, though dwelling in the Colony as British subjects, and after compelling some Hottentots or Gonas to join them,[50] attacked Ft. Beaufort, and swept off some cattle, and, it is feared, killed some people.

General Orders have been published to-day, appointing Col. Somerset as Commandant of all the Frontier Districts under Martial law, with the local rank of Major General. He is to collect at Ft. Hare all the Burghers and Levies from the Colony, and as soon as a sufficient force is there concentrated, a movement into Kafirland will take place.

It is reported that the Cape Corps soldiers stationed at Line Drift, were taken prisoners by Siyolo, who destroyed the post, and removed to his kraal.[51]

January 4th : Yesterday morning some firing was heard in the direction of Fort White, which induced the Governor to send out a spy to ascertain the cause. He returned with the information that Sandili had attacked that post[52] at the time specified, and that he was now endeavouring to collect his forces, and to decoy the troops out. Stock's camp was in the same neighbourhood. Some mule wagons came in safely from East London last night. Pato's Kafirs had escorted them in conjunction with a small party of the Cape Corps. With the exception of Siyolo, none of the Hlambie chiefs have yet taken any open part against us. Umhala has sent in word to Maclean that he shall sit still. Some of the people, it is said, are beginning to talk of the failure of Umlanjeni's promises.[53] This will probably have a good effect, and perhaps prevent many from hastily plunging into war. The Lord is merciful to us here. Although there must be some thousands of cattle in the place, yet we have hitherto had no attack.

January 6th: One of the two Fingoes who were returning to Peddie with a post from the Governor on Saturday evening, was murdered about five miles from Ft. Murray, and the bag with letters taken away. The other made his escape back to Ft. Murray. It is supposed that this was done by some of Siyolo's Kafirs. A herd of Cattle were taken by the Kafirs from the Flat[54] this morning, but were soon retaken by the Cape Corps and some of the Civilians, one of whom has been wounded in the temple by an assegai.

It is said that Sandili's brother Dundas was wounded in the back at the attack on Fort White.

January 10th: Official information has arrived that Hermanus attacked Ft. Beaufort on the 7th inst. on which occasion he himself was killed together with about 100 of his rebellious followers, including some Hottentots.[55] This and the failure at Fort White will probably dispirit our enemies, and should call forth our gratitude to Almighty God, who has thus interfered in our behalf. It is said that Hermanus sent his sons a short time since to Umlanjeni with a white man's head.

January 11th: Two companies of the 73rd Regt. arrived this morning and a few artillery men, by way of East London from Cape Town.

A man of the name of McNaughten[56] had a narrow escape last night from the Kafirs. He was saved through the intercession of one of them who happened to know him. His wagon and oxen were taken, but have been returned with the exception of 4 oxen through Jan Tshatshu who stopped them.

January 13th: Yesterday about 300 Fingoes arrived from Fort Peddie as one of the Levies about to take the field.

January 14th: From a few letters which have found their way here from Graham's Town, we learn that several murders have been committed in the colony, particularly in the Winterberg by Hermanus's people.[57]

January 16th: About 140 Fingoes went out this morning to bring in some Oat Hay from Mr. Birt's[58] station. On their return they were waylaid by some 300 Kafirs. The Fingoes attacked them, however, with such spirit that they soon fled, having 3 of their number wounded.

January 24th: The Fingoes and some of the Cape Corps had a smart encounter with about 600 Kafirs headed by Siyolo this morning. The Cape Corps from Line Drift were amongst the enemy, and fought on their side. About 12 Kafirs were killed and several wounded. On our side 1 Fingoe, son of Jama,[59] was killed, and 1 of the Cape Corps wounded.

Some heavy firing was heard last Tuesday morning, supposed to be caused by an attack upon Fort Hare.

January 27th: Letters from Butterworth this morning. They have been in great danger there since we last heard. Rili however had at last decided for peace, though Mr. Gladwin[60] has very little confidence in him, and is still on his guard.

Some more of the Cape Town levies arrived in the afternoon. About 1600 have arrived up to the present period.

January 28th: There was a good deal of firing last night over at Mr. Brownlee's station,[61] caused by some Kafirs firing down upon the Fingoes. No harm, however, appears to have been done. Davies's levy[62] arrived this afternoon from Graham's Town, bringing some portions of our back mails. There are about 300 men in this levy, so that we have now here a force of more than 2000 besides the military.[63]

It appears that Gen. Somerset's despatches have been cut off by the enemy, which accounts for no official intelligence having reached us in reference to the Fort Hare attack. We learn however from other sources that they had a severe contest at the time we heard the firing here.[64] The Kafirs were much cut up, losing, it is said, as many as an hundred men, whilst the loss on our side was 5 Fingoes.

February 1st: Supplies have been successfully taken to Forts White and Cox. Col. Mackinnon went on Thursday with about 2000 men and returned to-day.[65] They met with very little opposition. They destroyed all the Kafir kraals in their road.

February 3rd: Heard yesterday from Butterworth. They continue quiet. Mention is made of 5000 Zulus marching down in three divisions. The Governor received despatches in reference to them, the nature of which has not yet transpired.[66]

February 6th: A large patrol went off for Siyolo's country on Monday afternoon, followed by another on Tuesday morning before daylight. Both returned together this afternoon, bringing about 600 cattle with them. They met with no resistance, the Kafirs flying before them. They burnt all the kraals. They were hindered in their operations by the rain, which was falling more or less all the time they were away.

Toyise brought information of the disaffection of the Hottentots at Shiloh,[67] of which station they have now possession, the Missionaries having all left. We have heard also that the Hottentots of the Kat River, Theopolis, & other parts are all disaffected, and have openly joined against the English Government.

February 24th: Nothing effectual has yet been done towards bringing our unhappy war to a conclusion. Gen. Somerset has been reinforced by some burghers from Cape Town and elsewhere, and additional levies have arrived here. Col. Mackinnon was out a few days since, and had one severe engagement with a large body of Kafirs who attacked him near the Keiskamma.[68] The Kafir loss was considerable, whilst ours was more than usual. The Peddie Fingoes made an excursion into Siyolo's country, and succeeded in capturing about 400 cattle, including those belonging to the so-called Kafir prophet Umlanjeni.

February 28th: News reached us last night of the victory gained on the 22nd inst over the Rebel Hottentots & Kafirs at Fort Armstrong,[69] by Major Gen. Somerset and the Burghers. About 100 of them were killed, and upwards of 200 taken prisoners, besides 400 women and children. Amongst the prisoners two are said to be Englishmen.

March 3rd: Col. Mackinnon returned from another patrol yesterday. As usual he did nothing.[70] Lt. Col. Eyre, 73rd Regt. having struck off from the main body captured about 400 head of cattle and brought them in the day previously.[71] The Hottentot Rebels at Eiland's post had surrendered to Gen. Somerset.[72]

March 14th: Last week supplies were again thrown in[73] at Forts Cox and White. Col. Mackinnon took them with a force of 2,500 men. On returning from Fort Cox to Fort White they were attacked by a large body of the enemy, chiefly Sandili's men, who were driven off after about 1 hour's fighting, with the loss of 100 men and upwards, including 10 principal personages. On our side 3 were killed, and 2 wounded. Instead of following up this advantage, however, Col. Mackinnon marched on to Fort White, leaving the Kafirs still in their main position, which would of course give them the impression that he was retreating from them.[74]

This week two patrols have been made up the river[75] and towards Mr. Birt's station, but with very little success. Rather more than 200 cattle were captured, but there seems to have been very little fighting. A sad mistake happened amongst the levies, Capt. Bevel having been shot in mistake for a Kafir by his own men.[76]

Last night about 45 of the Cape Corps, 12 of the Graham's Town levy, and 5 men of the Mule train,[77] deserted to the enemy with their wives and chattels, including their arms. The garrison was under arms all night, as it was rumoured that Sandili was in the neighbourhood. This afternoon the Governor assembled the troops and levies, and disarmed nearly the whole of the Cape Corps detachment at present here. He also disarmed some of the Graham's Town Hottentot Levy.[78]

April 3rd: Since my last entry the Governor has been to Fort Hare and back. Whilst out he had three engagements with

the enemy and brought home about 700 or 800 head of
cattle.[79] In the different engagements it is supposed that the
Kafirs lost nearly 100 men. On our side 4 were killed and
6 wounded. Mr. Chas. Brownlee[80] was wounded in the leg
by the assegai of the enemy, but is doing well. A patrol went
out into Siyolo's country last week, and had a battle with the
Kafirs in that part, in which 30 of them were killed.[81]

Last Friday evening, 28th ult. a melancholy circumstance
happened in the death of Mr. James Brownlee,[82] who had
gone out with a few Fingoes to re-capture some cattle. They
were overpowered by superior numbers, and Mr. Brownlee
fell by an assegai wound in his back, which soon proved fatal.
His body was left by the little party, being unable to bring it
away as the enemy were too strong. A patrol went out the
next morning and brought it in, but the Kafirs had cut off the
head and carried it away. His remains were buried on Sunday
morning, attended by a large concourse of people, both white
and coloured.

Something more has turned up about some of the Hottentots. A Kafir mule driver has also been detected in holding
communication with Sandili. Various reports are afloat as to
the intention of Rili[83] & Umhala[84] in reference to their joining
the war. The news from Butterworth is not very satisfactory.
Some Hottentots who have fled in that direction are doing
immense mischief by spreading false statements. A party of
50 had destroyed a trading station near Rili's place, but had
not injured the person in charge.[85] They had likewise
threatened Butterworth.

1853

August 8th: A long period has elapsed since my last entry.
Then we were in the turmoil of war, which was carried on
with great sameness of character and mode of operation till
last March, when the new Governor, Sir George Cathcart,[86]
was enabled to make some sort of peace with the Gaikas.
About two years ago my health failed, and I went eventually
to the Cape and afterwards to Natal, from which latter colony

I returned to King William's Town last October. At the District Meeting[87] I was appointed to Mount Coke, to which Station the Press was also to be removed. This change did not take place till last week. On Tuesday last, accordingly, we left King William's Town, and arrived at Mount Coke, our present home. May the good hand of the Lord be with us here also!

Yesterday I preached twice at East London, where I trust good will be done. We have at present there 5 members and 1 on trial. A small Sunday School has been established.

1859

June 25th: Another and much larger break in my Journal. Nearly six years have elapsed since my last entry — years of peace and quiet through the blessing of God. My work has not been much diversified during all this period.[88] Most of my time has been spent in translating the Old Testament into the Kafir language. Last evening I completed the Books of Kings, which has brought this work to a conclusion. The whole Bible has now been translated into Kafir, and many portions previously printed revised. I have still to revise the Chronicles. When this is done and printed we shall have published here a complete and uniform edition of the Kafir Scriptures, besides several portions of the Old Testament in separate books.[89] I have great reason to be thankful to God for the health and strength vouchsafed to me in the prosecution of this important work. May His blessing attend it, and may glory to Him redound thereby in the instruction and salvation of many thousands of the Kafir speaking tribes!

September 1st: Last evening I corrected the last proof of the Kafir Bible, being the closing portion of the Chronicles revised for the first complete edition of the Old Testament. To-day the printing this edition has been finished, so that now we have the entire Scriptures in the Kafir language.[90] To God be all the praise! We commenced printing this edition in December 1854, so that we have had this work in hand a little more than four years and half. During this period the whole has been translated or former printed portions revised. The translators have been Mr. Dugmore for the Book of Psalms, Mr. Garner[91] for that of Ruth, and Rev. A. Kropf[92] of the Berlin Mission for Judges and the two Books of Samuel. All the other books have been translated by myself, and those which were printed before have been revised, as well as the translations supplied by Messrs. Garner and Kropf. With God's blessing and help I now intend to give another revision to the New Testament, which will probably amount to a re-translation of the whole.[93] May the Holy Spirit be my teacher and guide in this, and in all other undertakings, to which the Great Head of the Church may deign to appoint me.

Bro. Glanville[94] of King Wm's Town has resigned the Ministry, which throws the Superintendency of that Circuit on me till Our District Meeting in November next.

The last four years have seen wonderful changes in British Kaffraria. In consequence of a dreadful famine brought about by their superstitious killing of their cattle and abstinence from ploughing, thousands perished of hunger, whilst many more went into the Colony and other parts to get a living.[95] Their country is now partially occupied by European Farmers. We have still Siwani's[96] people and some of Jali's[97] in our neighbourhood, as also some large Fingoe villages, but nearly the whole of Pato's people have disappeared from the country. Very few of Umhala's people are left also.[98] Most of the Chiefs have been transported to Cape Town for some cause or other,[99] so that the power of the Frontier tribes for mischief seems to be broken at least for some time to come.

September 12th: To-day the longwished for Kafir New Testaments have arrived from the British and Foreign Bible Society.[100] May the blessing of God attend their circulation. To-day, also, I sent off a copy of the Old Testament to the Rev. S. B. Ben ie,[101] the Secretary, and likewise a copy to Sir George Grey, our late Governor.[102]

Notes and References

1. Rev. H. H. Dugmore, 1810–1897, an active translator who had long been connected with the mission press.
2. Rev. H. Pearse, ? –1862.
3. Rev. J. C. Warner.
4. The District Meeting began on 27 January 1848. Appleyard was to begin the reconstruction of Wesleyville, because Pato's tribe had been resettled there. He was to take the press and printing office with him. Apart from his duties at Wesleyville he was to preach at East London in rotation. He had only three scheduled services and one prayer meeting per week.

   There had been a great increase in the number of Fingoes in the vicinity of D'Urban, and Dugmore was stationed there. He was also instructed to proceed with his translating.

   While Appleyard was away in Natal the press continued to operate under different management, probably that of Dugmore.
5. Appleyard's father-in-law Archbell was probably ill at the time. He became supernumerary in 1848 because his work was telling on his health, and he never again worked on a full-time basis for the Wesleyan Missionary Society. See Minutes of the District Meeting, Graham's Town, 22 November 1848. Cory Library MS 15,023.
6. The District Meeting began on 22 November 1848. It was decided at the meeting to move the mission press to King William's Town because of its "central position to all Kaffirland". A residence for the Missionary and a building for the printing office had been bought, and a stone chapel 45′ by 20′ was in the process of being built. The chapel was at 1 Durban Street (Cory Lib. MP 293) and the residence probably in Berkley St.
7. According to the Minutes the number was 285.
8. Rev. J. Wilson, 1820–1891.
9. Rev. W. Sargeant, 1820–1896.
10. Wesley chapel is in Graham's Town.
11. The giving of presents to chiefs was part of Smith's policy.
12. This statement is ironical. The District Meeting was largely concerned with the disciplining of various ordained preachers. W. J. Davis, who was well known to Appleyard, had purchased land in Pietermaritzburg evidently for his own use. Davis was Deputy Chairman of the Natal District and as such had certain authority. Revs. G. Parsonson, I. Allison and W. C. Holden had been insubordinate to Davis on the grounds that he had rendered himself unfit for authority.

    Furthermore Allison was accused of other financial maladministration. J. C. Warner's resignation was considered at his own request because he doubted his vocation.

    Davis became supernumerary for one year as he had been injured on falling from his horse. Pearse was sent to take his place, and he was very successful in restoring tranquillity. See W. B. Boyce *Memoir of William Shaw* p. 221.
13. That is, to King William's Town. "At the same time an apprentice was added to the establishment, & some time after a binder, who is also competent to assist in the Printing Office when required."

    Appleyard's report on the Printing Establishment for 1849 reveals how much had been achieved. (These schedules should be compared with those for 1859 – see below, Appendix p. 145):–,

"I. Printing Office"

3	½ sheets	1st Lesson Book	3,000 copies		12 mo.
7	,, ,,	Kaffir Hymn Book	1,000 ,,		,,
3	,, ,,	Portions of New Testament	500 ,,		8 vo.
6	,, ,,	Psalms, New Translation	3,000 ,,		,,
1	,, ,,	Kaffir and English Dictionary	500 ,,		,,
42	,, ,,	Kaffir Language	400 ,,		,,
1	,, ,,	Kaffir Hymn Book, Scotch Edition also	1,000 ,,		12 mo.

4 pp. to complete Kaffir Hymn Book   1,000 ,,   ,,
1,000 Dutch & Kaffir Society Tickets
200 School Schedules
200 Circuit Schedules
500 Title pp. to New Testament
Sundry Circulars & Hand Bills.

II. Binding Department

350 copies Kaffir Hymn Book, Stiff covers cloth bk.
66 ,, Hymns, Prayers &c whole bound
33 ,, ditto extra 78 half bound
3 ,, Portions of Scripture 8 vo. half bound
1 copy Kaffir Language 8 vo. cloth extra."

[14] Only one copy was completed, as can be seen in note 13 above.

    J. W. Appleyard: *The Kafir Language: comprising a Sketch of its History; which includes a General Classification of South African Dialects, Ethnographical and Geographical: Remarks upon its Nature: and A Grammar.* King William's Town. Printed for the Wesleyan Missionary Society. 1850.

    The Kafir Language, as we shall call it, was very well received by the District Meeting. W. Shaw, *The Story of My Mission* pp. 551 & 552, quotes from the Minutes of the District Meeting of December 1849:

    "Resolved, – That we have seen with great satisfaction the completion and issue of Mr. Appleyard's New Grammar of the Kaffir Language; a publication highly creditable to the learning and research of the author, and which must become the standard Grammar of the language. We thus express ourselves without forgetting the high merits of the Rev. W. B. Boyce's Grammar of the Language, (*A Grammar of the Kafir Language* Graham's Town, 1834. – Ed.) which was the first publication that supplied the key to the intricacies thereof by its development of the principles of what its discoverer called the "Euphonic Concord". We confidently recommend Mr. Appleyard's Grammar as, in the main, a correct and philosophical exhibition of the principles and rules which govern this ancient and interesting African language, so extensively spoken upon the Continent.

    The manner in which the work has been printed and bound, at our printing-office, cannot fail to reflect credit upon that establishment; and the work itself is calculated to serve the Mission, not only as forming a valuable help to Missionaries studying the language, but also as suggesting useful hints to those on whom the duty and honour devolves of completing translations of the Holy Scriptures into the Kaffir tongue."

[15] Appleyard does not mention the District Meeting held at Graham's Town from 25 November 1850. He was present. He reported to the meeting that the printing press had produced 1,138,400 pages during the year.

[16] Smith left Simonstown on 17 October 1850 in the *Hermes*, landed at East London on 20 October and was in King William's Town the same day. He held a meeting of the

chiefs on 26 October, but the Gaika paramount chief Sandili and his brother Anta refused to attend. On 30 October Smith deposed Sandili, in his absence, and Smith assumed from the results of sectional meetings held by the commissioners with their particular chiefs that they approved of the deposition. On 18 November Smith left Graham's Town for Cape Town. Three weeks later, accompanied by reinforcements of the 73rd Regiment and 30 of the Royal Artillery, he embarked again on the *Hermes* and arrived at East London on 9 December. G. E. Cory *Rise of South Africa* Vol. V pp. 297-305.

17 On 16 December Smith offered a reward of £500 or 250 head of cattle for the capture of Sandili and £200 or 100 head of cattle for Anta.
18 Lt.-Col. Eyre took 389 men and 4 officers to Kubusi Nek.
19 Lt.-Col. MacKinnon took 571 men and 7 officers to Fort Cox.
20 Lt.-Col. G. H. MacKinnon, chief commissioner of British Kaffraria, 23 December 1847-October 1852.
21 According to du Toit, A. E., *The Cape Frontier*, 1847-66, p. 59, Councillors were appointed for the Gaika (Sandili's) tribe, eight by the Governor and eight by Sutu.
22 Mackinnon left on 24 December with 19 officers and 568 rank and file. Cory *Rise of South Africa* Vol. V p. 306.
23 Fort White had been established in 1835 and named after Major T. C. White of the Burgher forces. Fort White was situated at the source of the Debe river, near Ntaba Ndoda. A. W. Burton *The Highlands of Kaffraria* p. 31.
24 The garrison had beaten off a determined attack and their attackers had regrouped out of range of the guns. They disappeared when Mackinnon's force arrived. Cory (ibid.) p. 310, quoting Lt. Armytage.
25 This was known as the battle of Boomah Pass.
26 The bodies were found by Mackinnon's force on its approach to Fort White. There is disagreement as to the number of men killed: Sir Harry Smith's *Autobiography* Vol. II p. 74 agrees with Appleyard that there were seventeen altogether, whereas Cory, *Rise of South Africa* Vol. V p. 310 and R. Godlonton and E. Irving, *A Narrative of the Kaffir War of 1850-1*, Vol. I p. 51 state that the total number was fifteen.
27 The situation at King William's Town is summed up in Godlonton and Irving, ibid, p. 61, as follows:
"The situation of King William's Town was for two or three days most critical, – it was comparatively speaking defenceless. Here there was no artillery, a sad and unaccountable omission of even ordinary precaution. The circumstance of four hundred British subjects living in an open town, surrounded by thousands of semi-barbarians ... Colonel Eyre with his detachment fell back from the Kabousie Neck, upon King William's Town, on the 28th December, and by this timely reinforcement the town was in all probability saved from assault."
Communications between King William's Town and Fort Hare had to go via Graham's Town, and Fort Cox was quite isolated.
28 These must have been local volunteers: the burghers were not called out officially before 31 December, 1850.
29 The rebellion of the Hottentots was still in the embryo stage, but it had been observed in the Boomah Pass battle that some of the Hottentots and Kaffir police behaved questionably. G. E. Cory *Rise of South Africa* Vol. V p. 309.
30 Line Drift post was burned on 28 December 1850. Only the officer in charge, Sergt. Kelly, and the issuer of stores returned to Fort Peddie. Cory, Ibid. p. 322.
31 Rev. J. Niven of the Glasgow Missionary Society escaped together with his wife and four sons, Mrs. Niven's niece, Mr. Ball an English carpenter and a Xosa Christian girl Tause. They left their mission station, Uniondale, for the Chumie station, 22 miles away, on Christmas morning. They were deprived of their horses and

effects by different roving bands on the way, and their lives seem to have been spared partly owing to the influence of Tause, a daughter of Soga, who had been one of old chief Gaika's counsellors. Niven had compromised his traditional immunity from attack by helping Mackinnon's men, and Ball would have been regarded as fair game. Ibid. pp. 316–19.

[32] This section is crossed out in the original, probably because although it had been the intention of Niven, Rev. Cumming and Rev. Renton and their families to make Fort Hare, they were forced to stop at Philipton where they were under Rev. Read's protection. Ibid. p. 343.

[33] Unidentified.

[34] Rev. W. McDiarmid, of the Glasgow Missionary Society.

[35] Rev. J. Ross of the Glasgow Missionary Society.

[36] There were two Berlin Society Stations in Kaffraria.

[37] Probably Charles White, a catechist of the Wesleyan Society who was received as an Assistant Missionary on trial, at the District Meeting of December 1849.

[38] Pato, Dilima and the whole tribe had undertaken to guard the route from East London to King William's Town for the colonial authorities.

[39] Fort Murray was established in 1835, near Mt. Coke Mission station. It was a depot of the Kaffir police and the Wesleyans held services there in Xosa and English. Minutes of the District Meeting, 22 November 1848. It was also the headquarters of Capt. Maclean, then Ndhlambi commissioner.

[40] Tshatshu, Pato, Kobus, Toise, Umhala, Siyolo, Siwani and Umkye had met Maclean at Fort Murray and expressed disapproval of the prophet Umlageni and all his doings.

[41] According to Cory, 16 men died at Woburn, 22 at Auckland and three at Juanasberg, making a total of 41. *Rise of South Africa* Vol. V pp. 312–14.

[42] They were not killed.

[43] On 29 December 1850 Somerset sent a force of 150 of the 91st Regiment and 70 of the C.M.R. with one three-pounder gun to carry dispatches to Sir Harry Smith at Fort Cox. This force was attacked by overwhelming numbers of Xosa after it had travelled six miles. Cory states that 22 of the colonial force were killed and 20 wounded, but he does not estimate the number of Xosa dead. Ibid. p. 321.

[44] Sir Harry Smith had been immured in Fort Cox from Christmas day. According to Godlonton and Irving *A Narrative of the Kaffir War of 1850–1*, Vol. I p. 89, Smith broke through the siege "at the head of 250 Mounted Riflemen". He had "to run the gauntlet, as it were, for about twelve miles, a desultory fire being kept up for that distance by the enemy. On reaching the Debe Neck a strong effort was made to intercept him." He reached King William's Town via Fort White.

[45] The Kafir police had deserted from Fort Cox, taking the livestock with them. Appleyard seems to have the details almost correct but to have placed this action out of context. See above, note 43. There was no other attack on Fort Hare at this time.

[46] Unidentified.

[47] Toise was a Ndhlambi chief who had been hostile to the Colony in 1846–7 but was an ally in 1850–52.

[48] This was the monthly known as the *Christian Watchman*. By the end of the year its circulation was 700. Minutes of the District Meeting, 25 November 1850.

[49] C. P. Brownlee, Gaika commissioner in succession to Calderwood, who had his headquarters at Fort Cox.

[50] Hermanus lived in the Kat River Settlement. Soon after the Boomah Pass battle, on 28 December, he attacked Fort Beaufort. None of the defenders was killed on this occasion. Godlonton and Irving, *A Narrative of the Kaffir War of 1850–1*, Vol. I p. 94.

⁵¹ See above, p. 124 note 30.
⁵² Fort White was more or less under a state of siege until the end of January.
⁵³ See above, Introduction to Chap. V, p. 119.
⁵⁴ Unidentified.
⁵⁵ The engagement was of short duration, and ended soon after Hermanus' death. The attackers were pursued and their huts burned and cattle taken. Eye-witnesses agreed that about 100 of Hermanus' followers were killed, as does the General Order. Godlonton and Irving, ibid. p. 137–9.
⁵⁶ Unidentified.
⁵⁷ For details, see Cory, ibid., p. 322 & 330.
⁵⁸ Birt's station was Peelton, situated probably in the valley of a tributary of the Yellow Woods River, north of King William's Town.
⁵⁹ Unidentified.
⁶⁰ Rev. F. P. Gladwin, ? –1855.
⁶¹ Brownlee's station was close to King William's Town.
⁶² Lieut. D. Davies, previously superintendent of the Kafir Police based at Alice.
⁶³ Montagu, Secretary to Government, reported on 31 January 1851 that 2,650 volunteers were on the Frontier with 1,000 to follow. Cory, ibid. p. 325.
⁶⁴ See also above, p. 125, footnote 43. Appleyard seems on these two occasions to be referring to a single encounter.
⁶⁵ Mackinnon left on 30 January with 2,200 men, consisting of the 73rd Regiment, Hottentot levies, Fingoes and a six pounder gun. The wagon train numbered only 14, which were heavily laden. Cory *Rise of South Africa* Vol. V pp. 366–67.
⁶⁶ Smith had asked the Lt.-Governor of Natal for three or four thousand Zulus to attack the Gaikas in the rear. The plan was later shelved. Cory, ibid. p. 321 & 381.
⁶⁷ Shiloh is a Moravian Mission station, situated near the Klipplaat river about two miles south of Whittlesea. It was established in 1828 and the missionary at that time was Rev. A. Bonatz. On 25 January Hottentots from the station joined a large force of Mapassa's Tambookies (Thembu) in an attack on Whittlesea. Bonatz and his four brother missionaries retired to Whittlesea on 30 January. A long series of battles followed in which the Hottentots and their allies used the Shiloh station as a fort. Cory, ibid. pp. 347–50.
⁶⁸ Mackinnon began on a routine patrol on 13 February. He was attacked on 17 February, between Fort White and the Keiskama, throughout the day. Mackinnon lost eight men killed and seventeen wounded, and, according to his report, the Xosa suffered heavily. Godlonton and Irving, *Narrative of the Kaffir War, 1850–1*, p. 238–40
⁶⁹ Fort Armstrong had been abandoned by English and Dutch civilians under the authority of Commandant Groepe on 22 January 1851. The rebel leader Uithaalder, successor to Hermanus, took over the Fort which he used as his headquarters. Somerset's attack of 21 February 1851 was therefore against a British fort manned by rebels. After fierce fighting, the culminating point of which was a howitzer attack on the tower, the rebels who remained alive surrendered. Somerset gave various estimates of the numbers of the enemy dead, but it seems that the correct figure is 36. Somerset took 160 prisoners and there were about 400 women and children also connected with the defeated. See the reproduction of a painting of the attack in Cory, ibid. opp. p. 353. For the details of the attack see Cory, ibid. pp. 352–3. There is no reference to the Englishmen.
⁷⁰ Mackinnon started out with 2,100 men on 25 February en route to Fort White through Siyolo's country. He burned many huts and seven Xosa were killed.
⁷¹ Lt.-Col. W. Eyre was detailed by Mackinnon to take 700 men to form a camp on the

Tamagha river near Siwani's kraal. That task accomplished he rejoined Mackinnon, who then dispatched him with 1,100 men up the Umdigini river where he captured 400 cattle. Eyre returned to King William's Town on 29 February. Godlonton and Irving *Narrative of the Kaffir War of 1850–1*, p. 274–75, quoting Mackinnon's dispatch of 2 March 1851.

72 Eiland's Post is now the town of Seymour. 160 men were disarmed, but many of these were not rebels. Cory, ibid. p. 355.
73 "thrown in" means simply "delivered", in this context.
74 Mackinnon left on 5 March 1851. Appleyard's information is reliable but his adverse comment on Mackinnon's actions cannot be sustained. See Cory, ibid. p. 367–68.
75 i.e. the Yellow Woods river.
76 Captain Bevil of the Cape Town Levy. His death occurred on patrol and the report in the *Graham's Town Journal* states that Bevil's men were firing at an ox and he was shot as he came through a bush to stop them. He was reputedly popular among his men. *Graham's Town Journal*, 15 March 1851.
77 Cory gives only one number, and that is 46 of the Cape Mounted Rifles. ibid. p. 357.
78 Their arms were soon returned and the men placed on an active footing again.
79 Smith took the field on 18 March to investigate a report that Fort Hare was about to be attacked. He scattered a large enemy force. The cattle drive followed.
80 Brownlee commanded part of Mackinnon's force.
81 This patrol of nearly 900 men was led by Maj. Wilmot, R. A. Its aim was to devastate part of Siyolo's lands. Wilmot reported that "between thirty and forty" Xosa lay dead on the field after the first encounter. Godlonton and Irving, ibid. p. 305.
82 James Brownlee was son of Rev. J. Brownlee and brother of Charles. *Dictionary of South African Biography*, Vol. I p. 126.
83 On 14 April some of Sirili's men were found to be fighting in Mapassa's force on the Imvani river. Hostilities were commenced against Sirili in December 1851.
84 Umhala was subject to great pressure to join the Xosa war effort and his behaviour was often referred to as suspicious, but he was not directly implicated. cf. Cory, ibid. p. 452.
85 On 20 March Crouch's mission station, called "The Spring", was attacked by 30 Hottentots, and later the Hottentots urged Sirili to attack Butterworth. Cory, ibid. p. 377 & 378, and Godlonton and Irving, ibid. p. 273 & 307.
86 Lt.-General Sir George Cathcart, 1795–1854, Governor of the Cape Colony 31 March 1852–26 May 1854. Peace was concluded with the Gaikas by proclamation on 2 March 1853. The Gaikas were expelled from the Amatola mountains and settled near the Kei though still on the western side. For details of the terms see Cory, ibid. pp. 484–90. It was some time before all the new arrangements could be carried into effect.
87 The District Meeting began on 22 November 1852 in Graham's Town. The missionaries were not formally stationed anywhere in view of the uncertain future of the tribes. The meeting directed that the mission press be removed to Mount Coke, and Appleyard stated in his report on the printing establishment for 1853 that there ". . . its several departments have been carried on with less interruption and under stricter surveillance than at any former period." Minutes of the District Meetings of 1852 and 1853.

Appleyard complained that the press was worn out and the types ill-assorted and therefore he could not produce the quality which he desired.

88 By 1856 Appleyard's pastoral duties had been reduced to two "Preachings" per Sunday, and during the week his whole attention was to be devoted to the management of the press and translation of the Scriptures. Minutes of the District Meeting

89 19 November 1856. He did, however, participate in baptisms. Register of Baptisms, Mount Coke November 1848–February 1882. Cory Library MS 15,344.
89 For a complete list of the separate publications, with names of the translators and dates of publication, see J. W. Appleyard, *An Apology for the Kafir Bible: being a reply to the Pamphlet Entitled, "Rev. J. W. Appleyard's Version Judged by Missionaries of Various Denominations and others."* Mount Coke, 1867, pp. 8–9.
90 It appeared as follows: "Bound up in four parts, each of which was published separately, as finished. When finally completed, the work was bound up in two volumes, and sometimes in one." Concurrently separate editions of single books by various translators were published at Mt. Coke.
91 Rev. W. H. Garner, 1812–1864.
92 Rev. A. Kropf of the Berlin Mission translated the Bible himself in 1887–89. J. du Plessis, *Christian Missions in South Africa* p. 352, states his translation improved on Appleyard's.
93 Appleyard's reason for this was as follows:
"When I came to the New Testament, and began to compare the Gospels together, I found that, in order to carry out the plan which I had proposed to myself, it would be necessary, partly on account of the peculiar grammatical construction of the Kafir language, to re-write at least several portions. This plan was to make the translation uniform as a representation of the original, so that, for example, where the Greek was the same in the various parables and discourses of our Lord, as reported by the several Evangelists, the Kafir should be the same likewise, and where the Greek was different, the Kaffir should be also different. The New Testament, therefore, I resolved to re-write altogether, as being altogether more convenient both to the printer and myself." See Appleyard; ibid.
94 Rev. T. B. Glanville.
95 The Cattle-Killing or National Suicide of the Ama-Xosa of 1857 is famous. It began, as had the war of 1850–53, with a prophecy, and ended in starvation for almost one third of the Western Xosa.
96 Siwani had been loyal to the colonial authorities throughout the war of 1850–53.
97 Unidentified.
98 For the disposition of the tribes between 1856 and 1859, see the map opp. p. 110 of A. E. du Toit, The Cape Frontier, 1846–7, in A.Y.B. Vol. I, 1954.
99 For details, see du Toit, ibid. p. 104, footnote 139.
100 The association between the Wesleyan Missionary Society in the Cape and the British and Foreign Bible Society began in the 1830's, when Shaw decided that a press was necessary. The British and Foreign Bible Society made an initial grant of £1,000 towards a complete translation of the Scriptures into Xosa. Later grants included a large quantity of printing paper and £125 to defray the cost of binding. The edition referred to here is what Appleyard calls "New Testament, number 4" in his *Apology for the Kafir Bible*, p. 8.
101 Illegible.
102 Sir George Grey, 1812–98, Governor and High Commissioner 5 December 1854– 15 August 1861.

Bibliography

A. Bibliographical Material

Berning, J. M.: Index to Obituary Notices of Methodist Ministers, 1815–1920. Johannesburg, 1969.

Berning, J. M.: A Select Bibliography on the 1820 Settlers and Settlement. Grahamstown, 1970.

Cambridge History of the British Empire, Vol. VIII: South Africa, Rhodesia and the High Commission Territories. Bibliography pp. 917–1017. Cambridge, 1963.

Cory Library for Historical Research, Rhodes University: List of Accessions, No. 22 (Methodist Archives Collection). Grahamstown 1968.

Mendelssohn, S.: Mendelssohn's South African Bibliography, Vol. I. London, 1957.

B. Unprinted Manuscripts

Albany & Kaffraria, District: Circuit reports; minutes of district meetings of preachers (Eastern and Western), 1836–59. 3 bound vols., elephant. Cory Library MSS 15,704; 15,023; 15,024.

Ayliff, J.: History of the Wars causing the dispersion of the Fingoes. Cory Library MS 15,544.

Bechuana District: Minute book, 1837–56, including reports from the Stations (& schools), and circuits of the district. Bound vol. Cory Library MS 15,001.

Cape Archives: Colonial Office Vols. 445, 485, 511, 528, 540, 550, 565, 574. Lieut. Governor Series Vols. 344, 408.

Mount Coke Mission: Register of Baptisms, from 5 November 1848 to 5 February 1882. Cory Library MS 15,344.

C. Printed Official Sources

British Government: Parliamentary Papers, Correspondence re. Kaffirs, 1845–6. xxxviii [786]. London, 1847.

D. Unpublished Theses

Frye, J.: The South African Commercial Advertiser and the Eastern Frontier, 1834–47. Unpublished M.A. thesis, Rhodes University, 1968.

Schutte, P. J.: Sendingdrukperse in Suid-Afrika, 1800–1875. Unpublished D.Phil (Bibl.) thesis, Potchefstroom University, 1969.

Verwey, J. E. M.: Oorlog van die Byl: die Sewende Kafferoorlog, 1846–48. Unpublished M.A. thesis, Stellenbosch University, 1955.

Williams, D.: The missionaries on the Eastern frontier of the Cape Colony, 1799–1853. Unpublished Ph.D. thesis, Witwatersrand University, 1960. (2 Vols.)

E. Newspapers and Magazines

Daily Dispatch (East London): Supplement on "Peddie", 5 September, 1960.

Graham's Town Journal: 9 May 1846.

South African Christian Watchman, Vols. I & II, Graham's Town, 1846.

F. Printed Books

Appleyard, J. W.: An Apology for the Kafir Bible: being a reply to the Pamphlet entitled "Rev. J. W. Appleyard's Version Judged by Missionaries of Various Denominations and others". Mount Coke, 1867.

Ayliff, J, and Whiteside, J.: History of the Abambo (Fingos). Butterworth, 1912.

Bird, J.: Annals of Natal, 1495–1845. 2 Vols. Cape Town, 1965. (Reprint).

Bowker, J. M.: Speeches, Letters & Selections from important papers. Cape Town, 1962 (Reprint).

Boyce, W. B.: Memoir of Rev. William Shaw. London, 1874.

Brookes, E. H., & Webb, C. de B.: A History of Natal. University of Natal Press, 1965.

Burton, A. W.: The Highlands of Kaffraria. Cape Town 1969. (Reprint).

Calderwood, H.: Caffres and caffre missions . . . London, 1858.

Cambridge History of the British Empire, Vol. VIII. Cambridge, 1963.

Cory, Sir G. E.: The Rise of South Africa. Vols. II, III, IV, V. London, 1910–30.

Cory, Sir G. E. and others: Souvenir in Commemoration of the Centenary of the 1820 Settlers of Albany, n.p., 1920.

de Kock, W. J. (editor-in-chief): Dictionary of South African Biography, Vol. I. Cape Town, 1968.
du Toit, A. E.: The Cape Frontier, 1847–66. A.Y.B., Vol. I, 1954.
du Plessis, J.: Christian Missions in South Africa. Cape Town 1965 (Reprint).
Godlonton, R., & Irving, E.: Narrative of the Kaffir War, 1850–52. Cape Town, 1962 (Reprint).
Gordon, Dr. R. E.: Shepstone: the role of the family in the History of South Africa, 1820–1900. Cape Town, 1968.
Gordon-Brown, A. (Editor): The Narrative of Private Buck Adams, 7th (Princess Royal's) Dragoon Guards. Cape Town (V.R.S.) 1941.
Gutsche, Dr. T.: The Microcosm. Cape Town, 1968.
Hinchliff, P. B.: Calendar of Cape Missionary Correspondence, 1800–50. N.C.S.R., Department of Education, Arts and Science, 1967.
Jones, E. Morse: Roll of the British Settlers in South Africa. Cape Town, 1969.
Kennedy, R. F.: Africana Repository. Cape Town, 1965.
Lee, Sir S.: Dictionary of National Biography, the Concise. London, 1925.
Macmillan, W. M.: Bantu, Boer and Briton. Oxford, 1963 (Revised Edition).
Marais, J. S.: The Cape Coloured People, 1652–1937. Johannesburg, 1962.
Munro, W.: Records of Service and Campaigning in Many Lands, Vol. I. London, 1887.
Pollock, N. C., and Agnew, S.: An Historical Geography of South Africa. London, 1963.
Pettman, C.: Notes on South African place names. Queenstown, 1914.
Pettman, C.: South African Methodist place names. Queenstown, 1923.
Robley, H. G., and Aubin, P. J.: History of the 1st Battalion Princess Louise's Argyll & Sutherland Highlanders. (91st Regt.) Cape Town, 1883.
Sadler, C.: Never a Young Man: Extracts from the Letters and Journals of the Rev. W. Shaw. Cape Town, 1967.
Shaw, W.: The Story of my Mission in South Eastern Africa... London, 1860.
Smith, Sir H. G. W.: Autobiography, (ed. G. C. M. Smith). London, 1903.

Smith, T.: Memoir of Rev. J. W. Appleyard. London, 1881.
Theal, G. McC.: Records of the Cape Colony, 1793–1827. Cape Town, 1898–1903.
Walker, E. A.: A History of Southern Africa. London, 1957.
Whiteside, J.: History of the Wesleyan Methodist Church of South Africa. London, 1906.

Appendix

Report of the Printing Establishment, Mount Coke, British Kaffraria, 1859.

The principal event to be noticed in connection with this establishment over the year just closed, is the completion of the translation and printing of the Kafir Scriptures in one uniform edition, a work which has occupied a considerable portion of time and labour for several years past. Particulars are not specified here, as they have already been communicated at different times to the General Committee. In addition to the details usually reported, we this year append a comparative view of the publications which have been issued to our own and other Societies, together with a list of those which still remain in stock, in sheets and books, plus their aggregate value. [The price sheets have been omitted – Ed.]

(Signed)

Jno. W. Appleyard.

WORKS PRINTED

29 half sheets Vol. 1. Old Testament – 1,000 copies 8 vo.
1 quarter sheet Vol. 1. Old Testament – 1,000 copies 8 vo.
20 half sheets Vol. 2. Old Testament – 1,000 copies 8 vo.
1 half sheet Title Page and Contents to Vol. 1, Old Testament – 500 copies 8 vo.
1 half sheet Title Page and Contents to Vol. 2, Old Testament – 500 copies 8 vo.
5 half sheets Second Conference Catechism – 1,000 copies 12 mo.
9 half sheets Kafir Hymn Book – 2,000 copies 12 mo.
14 half sheets Dutch Hymn Book – 500 copies 12 mo.
11 half sheets Selections from Prayer Book – 1,000 copies sq. 32 mo.
1 eighth sheet Selections from Prayer Book – 1,000 copies sq. 32 mo.
12 quarter sheets Kafir Hymn Book – 1,000 copies sq. 32 mo.
25 half sheets Sunday Lessons Book – 1,000 copies 12 mo.
2 half sheets Book of Proverbs – 1,000 copies 8 vo.
2 half sheets First Spelling Book – 3,000 copies 12 mo.

48 half sheets S.A. Christian Watchman – 430 copies 8 vo.
2 quarter sheets S.A. Christian Watchman – 430 copies 8 vo.
12 quarter sheets Cover for Ditto – 400 copies 8 vo.
2 half sheets Covenant Service – 500 copies sq. 32 mo.
1 half sheet Tract on the Sabbath – 1,000 copies 12 mo.
1 half sheet Tract on the Sabbath – 2,000 copies post 8 vo.
1 half sheet Rules of Society in 3 languages – 550 copies 12 mo.
2 half sheets Articles of Benefit Soc. – 250 copies 8 vo.
1 quarter sheet Cover for Ditto – 250 copies 8 vo.
1,500 Tracts sheets "Indaba Erzilungileyo" (Good News) – 4 pp. 12 mo.
1,500 Tracts sheets "Igora Eliyimfama" (Blind Warrior) – 4 pp. 12 mo.
500 Titles to Vol. 2 Part 2 Old Testament – 8 vo.
130 Alphabet sheets – folio demy.
100 Sets English and Kafir Interlinear sheets – fol. 18 sheets the set.
50 sets English and Kafir Interlinear sheets – 4 to. 8 sheets the set.
50 List and price of Publication – 2 pp. 8 vo.
150 Office Invoice. Papers – 4 to. fscap.
50 Office Invoice. Papers – folio fscap.
3,000 Sets of Kafir Tickets.
1,500 Sets of Dutch Tickets.
100 Invoice Paper – Bible Society – 4 to. fscap.
500 Labels – for Kafir Bibles.
100 Book account Schedules – fol. fscap.
50 Blank Circuit Plans – bdside fscap.
175 Blank Circuit Plans – fol. fscap.
25 Circuit Plan – fol. fscap.
150 Receipt forms for Christian Watchman.
500 Errata. Vol. 2. Part 2. Old Test. – 1 p. 8 vo.
300 District Settlement and Estimate Forms – bdside fscap, ruled.
150 Circulars. Lovedale Seminary. 2 pp. 4 to. Post.
250 each Cards and forms of Admission to Benefit Society,
    making a total of
174 half sheets.
28 quarter sheets.
22 Sundry sizes.
    comprising 240 forms: 190,805 impressions, and
    1 eighth sheet. 1,696,065 pages.

BOOKS BOUND

1,907 First Lesson Book, 12 mo. stiff covers, cut edges.

1,313 Second Lesson Book, stiff covers, cut edges.
100 Reading Book. 12 mo. half-bound.
202 Bible Stories. 12 mo. half-bound.
300 Scripture Extracts, quarter bound.
504 First Kafir Catechism. 12 mo. stiff covers, cut edges.
400 Second Kafir Catechism. 12 mo. stiff covers, cut edges.
200 Kafir Hymn Book. 12 mo. stiff covers, cut edges.
200 Dutch Hymn Book, half-bound.
55 Dutch Hymn Book, 8 vo. half-bound.
44 Prayer Book. 12 mo. sheep.
436 Prayers and Hymns together – 12 mo. – sheep.
68 Prayers and Hymns together – cloth.
48 Prayers and Hymns together – 8 vo. – sheep.
2 Prayers and Hymns together – 6 half-calf.
97 Selections and Hymns together – sq. 32 mo. Roan.
200 Vol. 1 Part 1. Old Test. 8 vo. sheep.
100 Vol. 1 Part 2. Old Test. 8 vo. sheep.
300 Vol. 2 Part 1. Old Test. 8 vo. sheep.
300 Vol. 2 Part 2. Old Test. 8 vo. sheep.
100 Vol. 1 Old Test. 8 vo. sheep.
100 Vol. 2 Old Test. 8 vo. sheep.
624 Chronicles 8 vo. quarter bound.
189 Ezra &c. 8 vo. quarter bound.
771 Job 8 vo. quarter bound.
487 Psalms 8 vo. quarter bound.
147 Ecclesiastes &c. 8 vo. quarter bound.
152 Minor Prophets 8 vo. quarter bound.
200 Dutch Spellings 12 mo. stiff covers, cut edges.
150 Dutch First Catechism 12 mo. stiff covers, cut edges.
100 Dutch Second Catechism 12 mo. stiff covers cut edges.
104 Dutch Hymn Book 12 mo. half-bound.
490 Covenant Services sq. 32 mo. stiff covers, cut edges.
22 Vols. S.A.C. Watchman – 8 vo. half-calf.
4,800 Nos. S.A.C. Watchman stitched in cover, cut edges.
250 Articles of Benefit Society, stiched in cover, cut edges.
58 Vols. Of Sundry sizes and bindings
   making a total of
1,711 Vols. whole bound.
725 Vols. half bound.

2,670 Vols. quarter bound.
5,264 Vols. stiff-covers, cut edges.
5,050 Magazines, &c. stitched in cover and cut.

BOOKS COMPLETED

1,000 Copies. Vol. 1. Part 2. Old Test. 8 vo.
1,000 Copies. Vol. 2. Part 2. Old Test. 8 vo.
1,000 Sunday Lesson Book. 12 mo.
1,000 Second Conference Catechism. 12 mo.
2,000 Kafir Hymn Book. 12 mo.
500 Dutch Hymn Book. 12 mo.
1,000 Selections from Prayer Book. sq. 32 mo.
1,000 Kafir Hymn Book. sq. 32 mo.
500 Covenant Services. sq. 32 mo.
430 S.A.C. Watchman. Dec. 1858 to Nov. 1859.

WORKS IN PRESS

1,000 Copies Book of Proverbs.
3,000 Copies First Lesson Book.

PUBLICATIONS ISSUED FROM DECEMBER 1858 TO NOVEMBER 1859

	Publications	To Wesleyan Missionary Society	To other Missionary Societies
Kafir	Alphabet Sheets	80	7
	Sets of Reading Sheets	33	5
	First Lesson Book	1,561	671
	Second Lesson Book	498	204
	First Catechism	478	12
	Second Catechism	325	12
	Reading Book	113	6
	Bible Stories	64	36
	Scripture Extracts	263	7
	Hymn Book: 12 mo. Serr Ed.	286	6
	Hymn Book: 12 mo half-bound	108	24
	Hymn Book: 8 vo.	24	—
	Prayer Book: 12 mo.	1	24
	Prayers and Hymns: 12 mo.	420	18
	Prayers and Hymns: 8 vo.	35	—

	Selections and Hymns, sq. 32 mo.	33	—
	Old Testament: 2 vols.	82	5
	Old Testament Vol. 1. Part 1.	133	14
	Old Testament: Vol. 1. Part 2.	45	2
	Old Testament: Vol. 2. Part 1.	179	19
	Old Testament: Vol. 2. Part 2	188	20
	Psalms	246	156
	Chronicles	145	—
	Job	195	—
	Minor Prophets	61	—
	Portions bound together	33	3
	Tracts	300	200
Dutch	Spelling and Reading Book	150	—
	First Catechism	100	—
	Second Catechism	32	—
	Hymn Book	83	—
	Prayer Book	16	—
English	Alphabets	7	—
	Reading Sheets	7	—
	English and Kafir Interlinear sheets	3	—
	English and Kafir Vocabulary	14	1
	Covenant Services	100	—

Index

Abraham, 20
Admiral, 82
Africa, 83
Agent (see Diplomatic Agent)
Albany, 5, 27, 45, 109
Albert, Fort, 112
Aldum, 93
Algoa Bay, 120, 121
Amabala (also Amambalo), 69, 83
Amadhlambi (see Hlambi)
Amagqeka (see Gaika)
Amambalo (see Amabala)
Amapakati (see Umpakati)
Amatolas, 56, 67, 85, 87, 88, 89, 111
Amambombo, 123
Anta, 122, 123
Appel; Piet Appel toring (also Apple), 61, 99
Appleyard, John Archbell, 18, 19
Appleyard, John Whittle: Family matters, 3, 5, 9, 18, 82, 110; Journal, 27, 132; Illness, 10, 11, 107, 131; Kafir Grammar, 14; first preaching in Kafir without an interpreter, 20; in Colesberg, 27–32; witnesses battle of Peddie, 36; his involvement and accuracy, 36; prepares to flee from the Beka, 39; shelters in the fort, 42, 43, 64; rides out to witness an action, 67; qualities as a commentator, 79; interrogates prisoners, 81; sees surrender of Stock, 89; at Waterloo Bay, 95, 111; rides to Beka, 101; visits Somerset's camp, 105; appointed to D'Urban mission, 107; further advance in preaching without an interpreter, 111; rode to King William's Town, 112; translations, 119, 132, 133; at centre of Umlangeni war, 119; visits Natal, 121; stationed in Bathurst, 121; moves to King William's Town, 121; in charge of press, 122; visits East London, 121; prints Kafir Grammar, 122; visits Cape and Natal, 131; moved from King William's Town to Mount Coke, 132; becomes Superintendent of King William's Town circuit, 133
Appleyard, Mrs. Sarah Ann, 5, 8, 11, 15, 18, 19
Archbell, Rev. James, 5, 8, 9, 10, 13, 14, 31, 120
Archbell, James, 9, 10
Armageddon, 119
Armistice, 102
Armstrong, Fort, 15, 129

Artillery, 50, 52, 62, 63, 127
Ayliff, Rev. John, 2

Balata, 7
Barney, Capt. 60
Barracks, 47, 48, 50, 63, 123
Bashee, 88
Bata, 16
Bathurst, 49, 51, 121
Beaufort, Fort, 12, 15, 16, 19, 20, 29, 35, 41, 46, 48, 82, 90, 93, 96, 97, 99, 121, 126, 127
Bechuana, 27, 29
Bees, bee-place, 7, 17
Beka, mission station and river, 3, 5, 8, 9, 10, 14, 17, 18, 29, 32, 35, 39, 40, 46, 47, 53, 54, 64, 66, 83, 93, 96, 101, 110
Bele(Ama-), 2
Bell, 7, 101
Benjesi, 88
Ben i.e., Rev. S. B., 133
Beresford, Fort, 89, 90
Berkely, Sir George, 108, 109, 110, 112
Berlin Missionaries, 124, 133
Bevel, Capt., 130
Bible, 119, 132
Birt, Rev., 9, 124, 128, 130
Bisset, Lieut., 65
Block Drift, 42, 44, 45, 53, 56, 95, 102, 104, 108
Board of Relief for Distressed Fingoes, 62
Body-guard, 52
Boers, 9, 13, 27, 28, 31, 37, 58, 68, 87, 92
Boozak, 93, 96
Border, 9, 15, 39, 40
Botman, 35, 41
Boyce, Rev., 5
Brack river, 52, 55, 67
Breakfast Vleij/Vley, 65, 108
British Government, policy, etc., 2, 7, 15, 27, 28, 36, 41, 44, 86, 94, 102, 103, 105, 112, 122, 126
British & Foreign Bible Society, 133
British Kaffraria, 112, 120, 121, 133
British Kafirland, 103
Brown, Fort, 19, 45
Brown, Mrs., 124
Brownlee, Charles, 104, 126, 131
Brownlee, James, 131
Brownlee, Rev. John, 40, 42, 44, 70, 87, 96, 98, 100, 128
Buffalo river, 84, 86, 94, 96, 105, 106–7, 110, 121

151

Burgher Force, Burghers, etc., 40, 41, 48, 58, 64, 65, 67, 86, 102, 109, 110, 126, 129
Burns Hill Mission Station, 36, 46, 126
Butterworth, 8, 10, 98, 128, 129, 131

Caesar, 8
Calderwood, Rev., 95, 101, 103, 108
Campbell, Capt. C., 62, 66
Campbell, Major, 30
Camp (Military) formation of, etc., 70, 71, 82–4, 86–90, 92–7, 101–7, 110, 123, 126
Cape Colony, incl. Government, forces, colonists and colonial territory, 1, 2, 9, 12–15, 27, 31, 35, 36, 37, 40, 41, 43, 45, 48–9, 51–2, 53–8, 70, 71, 79, 82–6, 90, 91, 93–100, 103–8, 112, 123, 126, 127, 133
Cape Corps (see Cape Mounted Rifles)
Cape Mounted Rifles, 35, 37, 45, 49, 59, 60, 64, 65, 67, 88, 102, 107, 108, 119, 124–30
Cape Town, 14, 31, 40, 108, 122, 127, 128–31, 133
Cape Volunteers, 71, 81–2
Castray, 42, 43, 47, 93
Catechism on the Christian Religion, 101
Catechism, Second, 32
Cathcart, Sir George, 131
Cattle killing episode, 119
Cavalry, 1, 36, 37, 63, 65, 82
Ceded Territory, 103, 112
Census, 27
Chapel, chaplain, 5, 7, 9, 10, 18, 30, 31, 60, 63, 66, 68, 101, 105, 109, 110, 120, 121
Chiefs, 2, 3, 6, 40, 41, 48, 51, 58, 61, 68, 70, 79, 90, 92–4, 95, 104, 112, 119, 122–3, 133
Christians, 51, 104, 111
Chronicles, Book of, 132
Church, buildings and the Established Church, 8, 9, 17, 21, 31, 36, 42, 46, 111, 133
Circuit, 9, 133
Circulation, 133
Civilians, 127
Civil Commissioner, 101
Class meeting, 6, 11, 13, 19, 64
Clergyman, 8
Cloete, Col., 14
Coast (see Sea-side)
Coke, Mount, 4, 8, 9, 10, 20, 68, 87, 88, 93, 96, 105, 122, 124, 132
Colesberg, 27–32
Colonists (see under Cape Colony)
Coloured people, 104, 131
Commandments, 21

Commissariat, 1, 15, 36, 42, 48, 50, 68
Committees' Drift, 65, 85, 91
Conference, British Wesleyan, 18
Conference, peace, 91
Conway, 104
Council of War (see War)
Court Martial, 62, 66
Cox, Fort, 89, 119, 122, 123, 125, 126, 128, 130
Cradock, 29, 32, 107, 108
Cumming, Rev., 43, 44
Cumming, 68
Curlew (ship), 120
Custom, 6, 17, 18

Dacres, Fort, 82
Darrell, Capt. Sir Harry, 88, 112
Davies's Levy, 128
Davis, 59
Davis, Rev., 8, 14, 17, 120
Debi Flats, 86
Delagoa Bay, 14
Dhlambi/Dhlambie (see Hlambi)
Dilima, 39, 65, 66, 124
Diplomatic Agents, 2, 35, 90
District Meetings, 9, 10, 11, 14, 17, 18, 29, 30, 32, 107, 120–2, 132–3
Divine (Providence), 7, 17, 51, 53, 59, 63, 107, 111
Doctors, witch and medical, 7, 11, 18, 20
Donovan, Capt., 64, 67, 69
Dorrington, Rev., 121
Douglas (ship), 120
Dragoons, 7th Guards, 42–3, 45, 49, 50, 55, 58–9, 62, 67, 68, 88, 93
Drakensberge, 1
Drought, 10, 13, 15
Dugmore, Rev., 120, 133
Dundas, 127
D'Urban, Sir Benjamin, 1, 2
D'Urban Mission Station, 2, 39, 40, 42, 46, 83, 107
D'Urban, Port Natal, 107, 120, 121
Dushani/Imi-Dushani, 51, 58
Dutch, 10, 13, 27, 29, 30, 86

East London, Buffalo Mouth, 121, 126, 127, 132
Edition, 132
Eiland's Post, 130
Emigrants (of 1820), 3
England/English/Englishman, 2, 7, 10, 11, 14, 15, 18, 29, 39, 42, 44, 52, 54, 61, 65, 66, 83, 95, 107, 111, 121, 125, 129, 130
Eno/Nqeno/Qeno/Zeno, 15, 17, 67, 88, 91

Escorts, military, 36, 40, 43, 50, 54–5, 59, 60, 69, 71, 88, 90, 92, 101, 102, 110, 124, 125
Ethiopian eunuch, 111
European, 18, 51, 94, 111, 133
Eyre, Col., 130

Faku, 88
Falhein, 4
Fani, 51, 56, 58
Father, Heavenly, 18, 39, 47
Fatherland cow, 52
Fingoe, 1–3, 10, 36–7, 40, 42–9, 51–5, 57–8, 60, 62–8, 81, 83, 85–8, 93–4, 98–101, 104–6, 109–11, 121, 127–9, 131, 133
Fish river, Fish river bush, mouth and hill, 1, 2, 5, 19, 36, 43, 49, 52, 55, 59, 65, 66, 68, 70, 71, 82–4, 86–7, 89, 90, 92, 94, 99, 119
Flat, 127
Float, 29
Frank, Appleyard's cousin, 82
Fraser's Camp, 2
Fraser, Dr., 62
Frontier, 1, 2, 27, 35–6, 39, 45, 48, 79, 103, 112, 119, 133

Gaikas/Amagqeka, 12, 35, 40, 42, 56, 58, 87, 92, 95, 99, 101–3, 109, 119, 122, 125–6, 131
Garner, Rev., 133
Gasela, 70
Gcaleka, 1
General (see Berkely)
Giddy, Rev., 30
Gladiator (ship), 107
Gladwin, Rev., 128
Glanville, Rev., 133
Glasgow African (Missionary) Society, 43
Glenelg-Stockenstrom Treaty System, 1, 2, 35
God, 5, 8, 10, 11, 40, 43, 61, 63, 121, 127, 132, 133
Gonas, 126
Good Friday, 41
Gospel, 15
Governor Sir Peregrine Maitland, 13, 27, 31, 35, 41, 49, 69–71, 82, 84, 86, 88, 89–100, 102–5, 107
    Sir Henry Pottinger, 107–12
    Sir Harry Smith, 112, 120, 123, 125–6, 129, 130
    Sir George Cathcart, 131
    Sir George Grey, 133
Gqunubi river, 87, 95
Gqutsho river, 53
Graham's Town, 1, 5, 7, 8, 10, 15, 18, 19, 29–32, 35–6, 41, 48, 51, 54–5, 58, 62, 81, 84, 93, 95, 107, 108, 111, 120, 121, 127, 128, 130
Grammar (Xosa), 14, 29
Great place, 3
Great Trek, 27
Greek, 83
Green, Rev., 5, 40, 42–3, 46–7, 67, 70, 81, 101, 107, 108
Green river, 86, 88
Grey, Earl, Secretary of State, 79
Grey, Sir George, 133
Griquas, 27–8, 31
Gunukwebi, 2, 3, 35
Gwalana/Gualana river, 47, 59, 66, 70, 71, 82, 91
Gwanga river and Mission Station, 3, 4, 6, 8, 13, 17, 36, 48, 50, 61, 68–9, 82, 86–9, 90, 92, 100, 101

Hala (see Xala)
Hanisi, 68
Hare, 8
Hare, Lieut.-Governor, 13, 15, 19, 35, 41, 49, 53, 82, 86–9, 94
Hare, Fort, 124–6, 128, 130
Harvey, Sergt., 16
Harvey, 60
Haslope Hills, 15
Heathen, 12
Heaven, 52
Hebrew, 83
Hermanus, 95, 126–7
Hintza, 1
Hlambi / Hlambie / Dhlambi / Ndhlambi/ Jlambi/Amadhlambi, 2, 4, 12, 68, 69, 103, 122, 124, 126
Hogg, Capt., 84, 92, 101–2
Holden, Rev., 12, 15, 18, 32, 107
Holy Spirit, 133
Honour, his (see Hare, Lieut.-Governor)
Hospital, 1, 61
Hostages, 91
Hottentot, 10, 18, 37, 40, 44, 86, 94, 97, 101–2, 104, 119, 126–7, 129–31

Igqibira/Iqgibira river, 43, 100, 124
Imbuto, 2
Imi-Dushani (see Dushani)
Impey, Rev., 5, 8–10, 112, 120, 124
Independent minister, 121
India, 79, 82
Indian corn, 10
Infantry, 1, 43, 62, 65, 82, 89, 123
Interpreter, 16, 19–20, 85
Iqgibira (see Igqibira)
Irrigation, 16
Irura river, 83

Jack, 100
Jali, 133
Jama, 2, 128
Jamjam river, 85, 106
Jesus, 5
Jlambi (see Hlambi)
Johnson/Johnstone, Col., 86, 88–90, 92, 94, 97, 107
Jokwini/Njokweni, 2, 43, 49, 52, 57, 64
Joseph, "Old", 85
Joubert, Gideon, 29
Journal, Appleyard's, 79, 132
Journal, Graham's Town, 54
Judges, Book of, 133

Kaal Hoek, 16
Kaffar, 12
Kaffer, 7, 8, 10, 12, 14–18, 20, 29
Kafferland/Kafirland, 9, 10, 17, 45, 58–60, 63, 68, 82–3, 90, 100, 108–9, 126
Kaffir, 12
Kaffraria, 27, 120
Kafir (for details see under names of chiefs and tribes), 1, 21, 39–56, 59–71, 81–90, 92–6, 99, 100, 102–4, 106–12, 120–132
Kafir Bible, 132
Kafirland (see Kafferland)
Kafir Jack, 54, 57–9
Kafir New Testaments, 133
Kafir Scriptures, 132, 182
Kaloko, 6
Kama, 2, 3, 12, 90, 94–5
Kamastone, 32
Kat river, 16, 97, 129
Katshaza, 65
Kaulela, 2, 106
Kei river, 85–6, 89–91, 94, 103–4, 106–7, 110, 112
Keiskama/Keiskamma river, 1, 2, 4, 42–3, 47, 49, 60, 66, 68, 70, 84, 88, 90, 92, 94, 96, 98, 101–3, 106, 112, 129
Kidd, Rev., 39, 40, 44
Kings, Books of, 132
King William's Town, 1, 87, 107–8, 110, 112, 119, 121–2, 128, 130, 132–3
Kobi/Kobus, 12, 20, 41, 54, 56, 58, 69, 81, 105–7
Kok, Adam 11, 27
Kolbe, Rev., 30
Koonap river, 10, 16
Kota, 65
Kraals, 6, 7, 11, 17, 20, 35, 41, 44, 49, 51, 56–8, 66–7, 70, 86, 88, 92, 100–3, 126, 129
Kropf, 133
Kubusi river, 122–3
Kuze, 2
Kwelera river, 91–2, 95

Lama, 49, 52, 55
Language, 6, 14, 19, 29, 122, 125, 132
Levies, 37, 123, 126–30
Library, Graham's Town, 15
Lieutenant-Governor (see Hare)
Lime-kiln, 55
Lindsay, Col., 41–2, 48, 51, 61–2, 71
Line Drift, 60, 124, 126, 128
Lishuani, 30
Local Preachers, 9
Locusts, 7
London (Missionary) Society, 31
Lord, the, 5, 6, 8, 11, 13–4, 16, 18, 19–21, 39, 45, 47, 52, 60–1, 82, 92, 108, 125–6, 132
Lovedale, 102
Lower Albany (see Albany)
Lucas, 64–5, 67, 85, 105

Macdiarmid, Rev., 124
Macgregor, Dr., 54
Mackinnon, Col., 122–3, 125, 128–30
Maclean, Capt., 35, 42, 44, 53–6, 58, 63, 80, 84–5, 90–1, 96–100, 101, 103–5, 107, 109, 126
McNaughten, 127
Mabandla, 2
Madras, 79, 111
Maitland, Capt., 87
Maitland, Sir Peregrine (see also Governor), 35–6, 49, 51, 79, 82–3, 107–8
Mapassa, 92
Makomo/Maqomo, 41, 56, 86, 95–6, 99, 102, 104
Marn, 8
Marines, 82
Martial Law, 49, 51, 109, 126
Mati, 49, 52, 69, 81
Matomela, 2
Matyumzi, 43
Mauritius, 82
Mazeppa (ship), 13–14
Meat-eating (see Sabbath)
Members of Wesleyan Missionary Society, 6, 8, 16, 31, 42, 121, 132
Menzies, Judge, 27
Michel, Col., 109
Military (see Troops)
Military Settlers, 125
Ministry, 18, 133
Mission House, 7, 9, 47–8, 50, 60, 66, 83, 87, 93, 101, 110, 120, 124
Mission Press, 121, 122
Mocke, 27
Modder River, 27
Monro, Dr, 37
Morley, 8, 17

Mozambiquers, 94
Mule Train, 130
Murray, Fort, 124-5, 127
Murray, Rev. Jas., 30
Mutiny, 123

Na-Qayi (see Umkye)
Natal, 3, 8-10, 13-14, 27, 31, 107, 120, 122, 131
Natives, 11, 42, 94-5, 104
Ncinci, Martha, 70, 85
Ndamanti, 7
Ndhlambi (see Hlambi)
Ndywaro, 7
Nelson, 29
Neutral Territory, 94
Newspaper, 125
Newtondale, 3, 5, 46, 49, 50, 57, 68, 70-1, 92-3, 95, 97-9, 100, 101, 105, 107-8
Ngceleshe, 104
Ngwa, 7
Ngxasana, 7
Ngxoya, 7
Ngxumi, 7
Ngyogyo, 7
Niven, Rev., 124
Njokweni (see Jokwini)
Nkoli, 7
Nkulu, 7
Nmarantsi, 7
Nondyola, 7
Nonibi, 47, 55-6, 98, 100-02, 109
Norden, Capt., 102
Norris, 16
Norval, 29, 31
Nqeno (see Eno)
Ntambo, 7
Nurse, 18
Nxarune river, 94, 105
Nyulusi river, 94

Oat-Hay/oat-hay store, 61, 128
Old Testament (see Testament)
Oliphant's Hoek, 98
Orange river, 27, 29, 31, 112
O'Riley, Lieut., 16
O'Riley, Fanny Ider, 16
Oxford, 8

Pafa, 52, 81
Pai, 101
Palmer, Rev., 71
Parade Ground, 1
Paradise, 55
Paris (Evangelical Missionary) Society, 30
Password, 44
Pato, 2, 3, 6, 7, 12, 17, 20-1, 35, 39, 41-9,
52-6, 58-60, 65-7, 81, 83, 85-7, 95, 99, 101, 105-7, 109-112, 124, 126, 133
Patrol/e, 41, 68, 92-6, 98-9, 101, 104-7, 110, 123, 129-31
Peace, 90, 93-6, 99, 103, 105-6, 108-9, 112, 120, 128, 131-2
Pearse, Rev., 120, 122
Peddie, Fort; or "the Post", 1-4, 8-11, 14-16, 18-19, 36-7, 39-40, 42-7, 49-51, 55-60, 63-4, 66-7, 69, 71, 82-3, 85-6, 88, 90-1, 93-5, 98-9, 104, 107-11, 119, 120, 124, 127, 129
Philip, Dr. John, 27, 87
Philipolis/Phillipolis, 27, 31
Picquets, 63
Pietermaritzburg, 120
Ploughing, 95-6, 98, 133
Polygamy, 18
Port Elizabeth, 121
Post (see Peddie)
Post, "postmen", 36, 42-3, 51, 54, 57-9, 62, 95, 127
Pottinger, Sir Henry (see also Governor), 79, 107-112, 119
Presents, 122
Printing Press, 47, 119, 121-2, 125, 132-3
Prison/prisoners, 68-9, 81-2, 84, 86-7, 92, 95, 98, 102, 104, 123, 126, 130
Proof (copy), 132
Providence (see Divine Providence)
Provisionals, 81, 105
Psalms, 133
Publishing, 132

Qeno (see Eno)
Quarterly Meeting, 9
Queen of England, 103
Quota, 100

Rebels, 13, 122, 127, 129, 130
Regiment 6th, 102, 108-10, 123
7th (see Dragoons, 7th Guards)
27th, 86
45th, 31, 97, 123
72nd, 1
73rd, 110, 127, 130
90th, 66, 82
91st, 27, 31, 37, 42, 59, 60, 62-3, 82, 125
Registering System, 79, 103-8
Reledwane, 2
Retief, Post, 15-16
Revisions of texts, 132-3
Richardson, Col., 45, 51, 69, 89
Rifles (see Cape Mounted Rifles)
Rili (see Sirili)
Ross, Rev., 124

155

Rulu river, 105
Ruth, Book of, 133

Saba, 44
Sabbath, 6, 8, 10, 12, 15, 17–21, 29–31, 40–1, 54, 61, 111, 120
Sacrament, 8, 13, 41–2
Sailors, 82
Saint Simon & Saint Jude, 1
Salem, 5, 9
Samuel, two Books of, 133
Sandili/Sandilla, 12, 35–6, 41, 46–7, 53, 56–8, 67, 70, 88, 92, 96, 99–100, 104, 107, 109, 111, 122–3, 126–7, 130–1
Sarah, Appleyard's cousin, 8
Sargeant, Rev., 121
Saviour, 16
Scholtz, Rev., 54
School, 6, 8
Scotchman, 125
Scotland, 30
Scouts, 51
Scriptures, 17, 31, 119
Sea, sea-side or coast, 16–17, 20, 81, 84, 105
Seagram, Capt., 31
Secretaries, of Wesleyan Missionary Society, London, 8, 102
Services, 6, 10
Seyolo (see Siyolo)
Shaw, Rev., 4–5, 9–10, 17, 27, 39–41, 80, 94–5, 105–6, 112, 120–1
Shepstone, Theophilus, 3, 8, 12, 35, 88
Shepstone, W., 52, 69, 83, 86, 104, 109
Shiloh, 129
Shushu river, 97
Simka, 41
Sirili/Rili, 58, 85–6, 89, 92, 98, 101, 106, 112, 128, 131
"Sitting still", 41, 45, 47, 58, 83, 86, 123
Siwani, 65, 69, 88, 133
Siyolo/Seyolo, 45, 47, 55, 67, 87–8, 102, 106–7, 124, 126–9, 131
Sizaka, George, 64, 68
Smailes, Rev., 32
Small-pox, 20
Smith, Capt. C. J., 13
Smith, Sir Harry W. G. (see also Governor), 111–12, 119, 122
Smith, Rev. J., 18, 121
Smith, J. C., 61
Smith, J. J., 15
Smith, Major, 110
Smith, Sergt., 16
Smith, Rev. T., 17–18
Smith, "a Mr.", 92
Somerset, Lieut.-Col. (later Major-General), 48, 65–7, 69–71, 81–4, 86, 88–96, 100–2, 104–5, 107–12, 124, 126, 128–30
Somerset, Mount, 58, 65, 88
Sonto, 56, 68, 70, 107
South Africa, 94
Spies, 47, 51, 60, 62, 66, 70, 80–2, 85, 100, 126
Spirit, 21
Spochter, 85
Spoer, 49, 97, 100
Star Fort, 1, 2,
Station (Mission) Beka, 6, 8, 11, 14, 17, 20, 30, 36, 39, 53, 60, 63–4, 94, 99, 101
Birt's, 128, 130
Burnshill, 109–10, 124–6
Coke, Mount, 132
D'Urban, 40, 68, 81, 92
Shiloh, 129
in general, 47
Station, naval, 82
Sterk, 62
Stirk, 3, 111
Stock, 41, 44–5, 47–8, 55–6, 59, 61, 67–70, 81–6, 89–102, 104–5, 126
Stockenstrom, Sir Andries, 1, 2, 35, 89, 92–3
Stormberg Spruit, 30
Studies, Appleyard's, 83
Suicide, National, of Amaxosa, 119
Sunday School, 31, 132
Superstition, 11, 19, 133
Supplies, 36, 48, 62, 67–9, 83–4, 89–90, 95–6, 102, 128, 130
Suta/Sutu, 12, 123, 125

Tainton, R., 3, 6, 44, 64, 68, 81, 110
Tainton, R. (Jnr.) 50, 59
Tamara river, 55, 86, 88, 93, 97, 101
Taylor, Rev. 30
Taylor, Mrs., 30
Tembookies, 58
Testament, Old, 132–3
Testament, New, 133
Theopolis, 81, 129
Thomas, Rev., 10
Thompson, Rev., 31
Thompson, Rev., of Graham's Town, 121
Ticket Money, 6, 13
Tickets of Location, 103–4
Toise/Toyise, 125, 129
Tola, 35, 41, 45, 71, 107
Tower (see Watch tower)
Traders, 39, 40, 46, 50, 131
Translations, 132–3
Transvaal, 3
Troops (see also Burgher force, Cape

Mounted Rifles, Escorts, Fingoes, Levies, Provisionals, Regiments, Scouts, Spies, Volunteers), 15, 19, 30–1, 35–7, 41–9, 52–4, 57–62, 64, 66–9, 79, 83–91, 95–6, 99, 103, 105–7, 109–12, 122–3, 126, 128, 130
Trumpetter's Drift, 1, 48, 55, 58–60, 62, 65–9, 71, 81, 108
Trans-Orangia, 27
Trekboers, 27
Tshatshu, Jan, 87, 96, 98, 100–1, 104, 124, 127
Tshatshu, Mary, 87
Tsomo river, 89
Tua river, 96, 108–10
Tyumie river, 103, 124

Ubuvu, 7
Ufani, or Uhobosho, 7
Ugxehao, 7
Uhoma, 7
Uitenhage, 109
Ukelembi, 7
Ukobo, 7
Ukunene, 2
Ukwenkwezi, 2
Ulisiba, 65
Uman-Yanda, 54
Umatoyi, 7
Umatyumza, 7
Umbe, 7
Umboni, 46
Umbulu, 7
Umbulula, 7
Umhala, 2, 19, 41, 44, 46–7, 52, 57–8, 60, 67–70, 85–88, 93, 96, 99, 102, 105, 124, 126, 131, 133
Umkye / Umgai / Umkai / Um-Qai, 2, 4, 6, 7, 17, 35, 41, 44–8, 50, 52, 54–8, 60–1, 64, 68–70, 84, 99–100, 102, 105–6
Umlangeni/Umlanjeni, 119, 126–7, 129
Umlangeni War, 119, 126, 129, 131
Umpakati/Amapakati, 39, 101
Umpehla, 55
Umphala, 2
Umyanda, 64
Umye, 55
Umyisheni, 7
Umzaya, 101
Ungesi, 7
Ungqera, 7
Usali, 7
Utofili, 6
Utyala, 6
Utyali, 12
Utyutyu, 7
Uvana, 7

Victoria, district of, 112
Victoria, Post, 45, 60
Victoria, Queen, 27
Volunteers, 123

Wagons, 9, 42, 50–1, 55–6, 59–62, 65–71, 83–4, 87–91, 99, 101–2, 107, 110, 124, 126–7
Wagon road, 65
War of the Axe, 35, 37, 39, 41, 47, 54, 60–1, 68, 81, 84–7, 91–2, 94–5, 98, 102–9, 111–2, 119
War-cry, 43, 46, 48, 51, 54, 57
Warden, Fort, 107
Warner, Rev., 120
Wason, 8
Watchtower, 1, 3, 8, 48, 63
Waterloo Bay, 93, 95, 97, 107, 112, 120
Webb, 40, 58–9
Wesley Chapel, 121
Wesleyan Missionary Society, 2, 3, 5, 8, 27
Wesleyville, 3, 4, 9–10, 61, 68, 85, 95, 110, 120–1, 124
White, 124
White, Fort, 123–4, 126–8, 130
White man, 64, 104, 119, 127, 131
Wilson, Rev., 121
Willshire/Wiltshire, Fort, 48, 90, 93, 95
Winterberg, 127
Wright, 81
Wrongs of the Kafirs, 87
Xala/Hala, 69, 101
Xamli, 68
Xasana, 48, 52
Xmas Day, 123
Xosa (see also Kafir), 1, 6–7, 35–6, 39, 44, 46, 79, 81, 101, 119

Yarborough, Major, 41, 62, 82
Young, Lieut.-Governor, 110
Yoyoze, 7

Zeno (see Eno)
Zetu, 68, 70
Zizi, Ama-, 2
Zulu, 129
Zwartkopjes, battle of, 28